Critical praise for

THE LAST FINE TIME

"*The Last Fine Time* is about Buffalo in roughly the same way *Moby Dick* is about whaling....[It] is a brilliantly written place where nostalgia turns into a meditation on culture."
—*Buffalo News*

"Celebrates both a collective feeling and an era in the history of cities now vanished...What reader can resist such gorgeous writing?"   —*The New York Times Book Review*

"Verlyn Klinkenborg belongs to a select company of writers —among them Tracy Kidder, John McPhee, Jane Kramer and Richard Rhodes—who...take non-fiction as seriously as great fiction....*The Last Fine Time* paints a graceful, elegiac portrait of blue-collar America as reflected in the mirror behind the bar of [a] corner tavern."
—*Cleveland Plain Dealer*

"*The Last Fine Time* is a touching memoir, a verbal snapshot that contains more truth than any historian could cram into a book twice the size." —*Detroit Free Press*

"Compelling reading."   —*Chicago Tribune*

"The story of George and Eddie's is the story of America. ...*The Last Fine Time* is a great portrait of America and of how far we've all come from corner bars and parish churches."   —*Kansas City Star*

"A helluva fine read...an evocative piece of social history."
—*Philadelphia Inquirer*

ALSO BY
VERLYN KLINKENBORG:

Making Hay

THE
LAST FINE
TIME

Verlyn Klinkenborg

VINTAGE BOOKS
A DIVISION OF RANDOM HOUSE, INC.
NEW YORK

FIRST VINTAGE BOOKS EDITION, FEBRUARY 1992

Copyright © 1990 by Verlyn Klinkenborg

All rights reserved under International and Pan-American
Copyright Conventions. Published in the United States by
Vintage Books, a division of Random House, Inc., New York,
and simultaneously in Canada by Random House of
Canada Limited, Toronto. Originally published in hardcover
by Alfred A. Knopf, Inc., New York, in 1991.

A portion of this work was originally published in somewhat
different form in *The New Yorker.*

Library of Congress Cataloging-in-Publication Data
Klinkenborg, Verlyn.
The last fine time / Verlyn Klinkenborg.
p.   cm.
ISBN 0-679-73718-9
1. Polish Americans—New York (State)—Buffalo—Biography.
2. Buffalo (N.Y.)—Biography.   3. Wenzek family.   4. Buffalo
(N.Y.)—Social life and customs.   5. Hotels, taverns, etc.—
New York (State)—Buffalo.   I. Title.
[F129.B89P75   1992]
974.7'970049185—dc20   91-50207
CIP

Book design by Anthea Lingeman

Manufactured in the United States of America
10 9 8 7 6 5 4 3 2 1

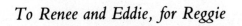

To Renee and Eddie, for Reggie

Buffalo is not a snobbish city. There is no city where solid wealth is more sincerely respected.

EBENEZER CARLETON SPRAGUE

Contents

PROLOGUE · *3*

EDDIE · *10*

THOMAS · *35*

JULIA · *65*

ARARAT · *88*

EDDIE · *118*

AN INNOCENT POPULATION · *149*

THE FALLS · *175*

EPILOGUE · *199*

NOTES · *203*

ACKNOWLEDGMENTS · *211*

THE
LAST FINE
TIME

PROLOGUE

Snow begins as a rumor in Buffalo, New York. The local television newscasters report it at noon, six, and eleven. To predict the possible path of winter's first storm, weatherpersons use live radar maps and pointers and an exchange of sober looks with the camera. Radio stations —even hard-rock channels—mention the oncoming snow at least once every five minutes throughout the day. The more sedate stations, the ones that play Sinatra and Tommy Dorsey back to back, update their audiences with reminders about emergency snow routes and the warning signs of frostbite and the proper method of shoveling walks. The weather is a subject well covered here in the Niagara Frontier.

But it is the mood that makes a snowstorm, and the mood in Buffalo begins as a rumor. The elderly put their heads together and fret: this is the time of year when parking lots are like bathtubs without handholds or rubber safety mats. This is brittle-hip season. Cashiers at the cavernous Bell's and Wegman's supermarkets around town swap weather gossip with their customers over the barcode readers at every checkout aisle, over the toaster waffles, the low-salt Swiss cheese, the toothpaste in the family-size pump dispenser, the $243.61 of groceries minus ten minutes of coupons pulled one by one from a soft-sided coupon file. The girls at Poise N'Ivy, a fashion boutique on Main Street in Williamsville, talk about snow with no less fervor and foreboding than do the boys next door at Bert Sweeney Men's Clothing or the skeleton crews down at the grain elevators beside the Buffalo harbor or the carpenters raising condominiums and luxury homes in what used to be woods along Transit Road out toward Lockport. From their glassed-in showrooms on Transit Road itself, auto salesmen watch the weather laying itself in from the west, the clouds like a field of gray tumuli, the remnants of a mound-building people. At Ted's Charcoal Broiled Red Hots restaurants across the city and at John & Mary's A-Bomb Subs as well, there is electricity in the lunch lines that form in front of the sizzling grills and the cash registers. Only in the covered malls, where the dreary sky makes no impression, does the mood of anticipation fade.

The carwashes prepare for extra business, for drivers who will soon be coming in regularly to remove grime and salt from their undercoated cars. The corner gas stations have already winterized most of their regular customers, but some people always wait till the last minute to put on the snows, till that first sickening unpowered drift into an intersection. At the greenhouses and nurseries, the memory of spring is buried as deep as a tulip bulb. The autumn leaf season is just over. Poinsettias will begin arriving in truckloads before long, and Land O'Trees, next door to Dickie's Donuts at the corner of Cayuga and Wehrle, will become exactly that—a lot so thick with conifers and the smell of pitch and pine that you might imagine yourself in the Rockies or the Alps or the Carpathians.

The first flake appears and vanishes like a virtual particle in the mind of a physicist. It might have appeared high over Our Lady of Victory Basilica in Lackawanna or above the Buffalo Lighthouse at the Coast Guard base on Lake Erie; over Martin Luther King Jr. Park or in the vicinity of the black-tongued bison at the Buffalo Zoo. It might have appeared anywhere. But suddenly, without seeming to begin, the sky is full of real particles falling so slowly that they appear to stand, wavering, in air. Suddenly the mood shifts. Snow is falling. Well. It is a relief, somehow. It is an event. It is something. It could be worse. All across the city, people stand at their windows. Throughout the day, shut-ins will tug at curtains, lift blinds to see if the weather holds. Office workers will find themselves watching hypnotically, admiring amid all the whiteness the dull green rosettes of grass that form at the bases of bushes and trees.

Eddie Wenzek is ready. Eddie Wenzek is always ready. He has had the blower tuned and the Chrysler Fifth Avenue winterized. The air conditioner has been sealed and the storm windows are up. Eddie has lived in Buffalo for all of his seventy years, and he has never owned snowgear more serious than a snap-brim hat, a London Fog topcoat, and a pair of rubbers. That is the point of living in a city. Had Eddie become a forest ranger, as his father once recommended, he might have needed Snow-Pacs and a parka, a chainsaw and a husky dog. Here there are sidewalks.

There are heated automobiles. There are snowblowers to open paths for Eddie's feet. There are the plows of the City of Buffalo and the plows of the New York State Thruway Authority. There are proud men who own four-wheel-drive pickups equipped with bright yellow Fisher snowblades and bug-eyed lights projecting above them. Eddie Wenzek has no small faith in the fruits of civilization.

All afternoon snow falls with the same patient accumulation that time demonstrates. By two-thirty, people are knocking off work, heading home before the driving gets much more difficult. Buffalo is a flat city, and at the overpasses where the Youngmann Expressway or Interstate 90 or the New York State Thruway rises above grade, there are kids sledding down inclines. Young mothers whisk their children outside to make snowmen. Some take to cross-country skis in Delaware Park or along the fairways of the Grover Cleveland Golf Course. Buses chink past, already chained up. Snow blinds the traffic lights, pastes the west sides of trees, obscures all the street signs that mark north-south avenues. Everywhere there is the low rumble of heavy treads on cleared pavement, the hissing of slush as it sprays off fenders and parked cars and pedestrians.

As light fades, then disappears, the balance tips in favor of the storm. Traffic on surface streets drops to a minimum. But on the Thruway, the rush of trucks and cars and the persistent scraping roar of plows, spreading loads of salt and sand as they go, keep the road open. Tandem-trailer rigs kick up blizzards of their own as they bear down on Buffalo from Boston and Schenectady and Utica. Toll-takers at the Williamsville toll booth, the last stop coming in from the east, see a steady decrease in business. They sit in their lighted cubicles, listening to the radio (where the talk is all weather talk now), and look out on the storm. A state trooper pauses to chat. Now and again a pair of headlights comes barreling out of the agglomerating flakes in the distance and gears down, gears down, exhaust belching, on the long approach to a full stop. Passenger cars creep down the off-ramps at interchanges far from the city and pull into motels, their drivers lucky by now if they find a vacancy.

By ten o'clock at night, the Niagara Frontier is shut tight, and yet this is no more of a storm than every winter brings all across the Great Lakes. The airport closed at seven o'clock. Transport has ground to a halt. The only thing open is the Niagara River, and that is not navigable in this season. Even indoors, you can hear the hush over Buffalo. You can feel the way the heavy snowfall changes a room, the way it redefines the interior, making the walls seem closer together, the roof heavier, the insulation thicker, as if the house had been built of logs and chinked with sphagnum moss, as if you might wake up in the morning and find the windswept tracks of lynx and snowshoe rabbit running down the middle of the street, as if the street itself were a frozen lake ringed by a forest of dark hemlock and spruce.

If you were the last person buying gas on a night like this, you would look up at the streetlamp overhead as you waited for the tank to fill with unleaded. You would see beyond it a ceiling—not a sky—of utter opacity, as black as the pupil of an owl's eye, out of which falls a globe of swirling snow. You would look at that owl's pupil, and you would readily imagine that there was nothing behind it, no moon or stars illuminating the tops of the clouds the way the streetlamp illuminates the snow on the ground. Nothing. You would stare into that owl's pupil of a night, and you would be the first to blink. You would pay the cashier watching a tiny TV in his sealed booth, and you would drive away toward a predictable source of warmth as fast as the snow would let you. When the wind blows off the lake, it can be hard to remember that close to earth is where the warmth is found. It can be hard to remember that the present is the only campfire in the icy wastes of time.

Eddie Wenzek is napping, the TV yapping away not far from the footrest of his recliner. The lights are dim. Eddie's wife, Renee, is in another room under brighter light, hemming a skirt, taking in a pair of slacks while she looks at a different picture on a different television set. If you happened to be visiting Eddie and Renee and you came in late after stopping for gas on your way home from a different neighborhood, Eddie would wake up as you entered the room. For a moment he would stare in confusion at the picture in front of him—a woman in a bikini pointing a gun at a man wearing a turtleneck—before snapping it off and saying, "Can I make you a drink?"

Eddie Wenzek is seventy, but he looks ten years younger. His forehead is round and high, his face open, though his eyes are small. There is a keen, inarticulate patience in his gait, a sense of waiting—for what, is not clear. He is not a large man, though the years have added girth to his beltline, which is set high on his true waist instead of his hips. For breakfast most mornings he eats a ham sandwich with a generous slice of last night's dessert. It is a habit from the old days when he used to get up at noon and go to bed at 4 A.M. Eddie is an exceptionally neat man. He may dress casually—an open collar, a pair of plaid pants—but he always dresses fastidiously. He pours a very stiff Scotch for his guest and an equally stiff Manhattan for himself. He wipes down the counter with a towel, rinses the mixing spoon, and places it in the dishwasher. He restores the bottles to their shelf in the closet. He takes one more look at the snow falling in the night outside and carries the drinks and two napkins to the kitchen table. The light falls from overhead on a basket of silk vegetables.

A silent toast. Glasses raised. There is a lean winter night proceeding unseen outside. The lynx and the snowshoe rabbit are running. The caribou are bedded down. Somewhere a wolf calls. Another answers. Beyond the streetlamp in the near distance outside the kitchen window, above a city that has been frozen into stillness, the owl's pupil stares. Snow falls and falls.

Eddie drinks, his guest drinks, and as they drink Eddie leans toward a story. It is his natural posture. He sets his glass down, empty, and this is how he starts. He opens his mouth and these are the words he uses:

"Say you're me."

EDDIE

Say you're me.

Eddie Wenzek

The bar's address was 722 Sycamore Street. Insurance atlases of the period—immense bound volumes that plot the distribution of indemnity and risk—record it as a two-and-a-half-story wood-frame building on a corner lot 36 feet wide by 106 feet deep. For the East Side of Buffalo, New York, there seem to be, in that incendiary index, whole chapters of two-and-a-half-story wood-frame buildings, all rendered in outline from a simulated aerial view, all, to an insurer, at equal hazard. These maps reduce a city to a survey of fuels, an infernal menu; stiff as vellum with pasted-in corrections, they are annotated from the flame's point of view. The pages crackle—the sound of fat in a very hot fire—as you turn them over on a table in a building deemed, by underwriters, unlikely to burn.

To all appearances these maps are the work of some compulsive hobbyist who is torn between the order of the city he has drawn and the arsonous disorder he imagines overwhelming it. And yet, despite their lunatic simplicity, it is impossible not to be moved by them. Here, from some supernal height, is visible the universal grid of urban living, as delicate a tracery as the lace on a christening gown. The tiniest squares are houses, every house an invisible suite of rooms through which daylight crawls and the smells of cooking percolate like moods. The feeling they stir comes from knowing that private life is a grave of incident—once lived, soon forgotten—and from trying to imagine the incidents of so many private lives without submitting to generalities. It is a feeling like compassion, but it also resembles the faith that existence is too varied, too ample, to be contained.

Insurance atlases of the period do not record the presence of large, graceful trees in East Buffalo or the way the streets were edged with square stone curbs, whose cutting and laying were the fiefdom of a potent Italian union. They do not mention the bricks that ran between the streetcar tracks or the rumble they caused when trucks turned across them or the slithering roar of the streetcars themselves. They say nothing about the markets and the parks and the dusty shopfronts. Nowhere do you find it written that this was a part of town where a woman's hands smelled different every day of the week—lye soap one morning, the next morning flour. From their commentary it is impossible to learn how the acres of two-and-a-half-story wood-frame houses that rose up like a climax forest years ago had long since cohered into a Polish neighborhood where each house was bound to those around it by an incalculable, and undelineable, number of associations—associations that in many cases reached back past the Atlantic voyage, past the crowded North Sea docks and their rail connections, and into the absorbent landscape of the partitioned Old Country itself. According to insurance maps, the only thing the houses of the East Side could communicate was flame.

They do not even mention that 722 Sycamore Street was a bar.

Much, then, will need to be imagined.

Imagine, for instance, a German steamfitter named Graf in a year let us call 1947. Steamfitting is the trade—the mystery—of welding fire to water, of causing steam to disperse its radiance along courses charted for it within walls and under floors until it surfaces in a radiator where a housewife puts dough to rise or sets a cakepan of water to ward off the prickling of skin. (Imagine the furlongs of steamfit pipe elbowing, knuckling, nippling its way through every building in a city like Buffalo that year, pipe mostly taking the path a rat would take in the daylight.) Steamfitting is dirty work, but Graf's gloves were always as clean as a doctor's hands. No one knows how. He worked hard, but never overtime—only enough to keep his wage from suffering an inefficiency, a loss of heat in the form of taxes to Uncle Sam. One hopes the undertaker knew a methodical man when he saw him.

Graf married a manufacturer's daughter named Isabel from Springville, New York, where—imagine—her father's house sat on a slope, defying the economic gravity that pulled factories and railways onto the valley floor. Graf put Isabel on the bus for visits home and never went himself, preferring to in-laws the company of the parakeet called Pretty Boy, which he and Isabel kept in a cage on

the icebox. Graf loved opera too, to the surprise of his
friends. The same friends said he looked like a thin Paul
Whiteman (but without the mustache) and thus a decade
and more out of date.

Of all the beers in Buffalo, Graf drank Ballantine's ale,
from Jersey. Not every day, and not immediately after the
job like shiftworkers given license by the coming of five
o'clock. Home first, dinner, then he and Isabel walked
through the elm-shaded streets of East Buffalo, it being
summer, and took a table in the front room of 722 Sycamore Street. They were served by a youthful bartender
wearing a white shirt—his second of the day—as clean as
a German steamfitter's gloves. The women there were all
well-dressed, and all the men wore ties, except for a table
of older men playing euchre under the front window,
through which the day's last light beyond Lake Erie could
be seen reflected in the panes and on the porch posts of
the houses across Sycamore Street.

One such night, taking a seat at the table, the bartender
put a question to the steamfitter. Would he install a new
boiler in the building? To Graf, so chary of earnings, it
was an imposition and a courtesy at once. The bartender's
logic was obvious. Steamfitters were plentiful in Buffalo,
but a steamfitter of such meticulousness, a steady customer, a Ballantine's man?

The old boiler had been a paragon since 1933, when,
except for its façade, 722 Sycamore was almost totally
rebuilt. A conveyor belt fed buckwheat coal into a conical
burner, and as the fire burned, the ash rose upward like a
powder-gray blossom. It was knocked off the top of the
cone by a rotating bar, drawn down suction vents, and
dumped in a pair of cans. But now fine ash flew up the
chimney and floated down on nearby houses to the east.
It was not as bad as the days they smelted at the steel plants

in Lackawanna, when women there breathed lightly and threw up their hands in frustration, but it was not a snow one wanted on the linens.

Graf agreed. He would consider the job. One evening he paced the pipes in the building, inspected the boiler, and counted the radiators.

"Twenty-three," said Graf.

"You missed one," said the bartender. "Come with me."

They walked from the barroom (two radiators under the front window) past the men's room (one radiator), the ladies' room (one), and a small dining room (one). Under the stairs of the family entrance (one plus the thirteen above), through the back dining room (four), and past the bandstand (none) they walked. The bartender opened a door in the middle of the back wall and the two men stepped into the garage.

It being summer, the effect was muted. So, imagine this happened in winter. It was snowing like mad. You couldn't see across the street. The air over Buffalo was a chill gray gelatin. Graf stiffened his shoulders against the cold as they crossed the threshold. But the garage was not cold. The bartender lit the room and the first thing Graf saw, after the gleam of a 1947 Pontiac 8, was an immense cast-iron radiator hissing on the wall nearest the door. The Pontiac was warm to the touch, as a new Pontiac should be, though it had not been driven at all that day.

But even in summer it made Graf smile. A radiator in the garage! Such a simple luxury—so well concealed! Exactly the indulgence to make a steamfitter smile! What was a postwar Pontiac but a piece of elaborate pipework with an excellent wax job? What finer kinship could there be between cast iron and rolled steel than the exchange of heat? What greater tribute could you pay to an automobile than to drive it off the salt-strewn winter streets of Buffalo (as well as out from under its bird-drop-raining trees) and into this fair harbor? In Graf's mind a new respect was born for the bartender's father, whose contrivance this was, and he said, or one imagines him saying, "I'll do it. But someone else has to tear out the old boiler."

And so the basement of the bar on the northwest corner of Sycamore and Herman streets was laid open that summer. The coal room languished in unaccustomed light. A neighbor drained the heating system and carted away the boiler in an ancient truck for free (leaving a trail of rust, which the bartender swept off the sidewalk with a stiff broom), for those were the days when after a week of inhaling coal dust, you would still call it profit to acquire a load of scrap iron. The bartender, himself a fastidious man, came down to clean and hang worklights before Graf arrived and to admire the surprising cavity where the furnace had stood whose ashes he and his older brother as boys had hauled to the beer drop and up out onto the street. Instead of coal, there would now be a gas fire: ashless, canless, boyless. Progress is so often revenge on the past.

The bartender was Eddie Wenzek, twenty-seven years old, born to Buffalo and the business. For Eddie one would like to claim everyman status, if that did not somehow demean him. One would like to find a permanent pose for him, a sculptural balance of muscle and bone that mirrored the inner arrangement of the man in 1947. One might stop him as he waxed the Pontiac or as he waxed his shoes or as he deplored the fact that new suits need not be waxed. He might be caught standing quietly on an autumn afternoon in the corner doorway, looking out at the intersection of Sycamore and Herman or at Witczak's Grocery—no larger than a pantry—across the street. He might be fixed in the act of pouring a beer or ringing up change or simply relaxing, enjoying a narrow pause in the fervor of a long night's work, his customers pacing themselves, his tailbone lodged against the backbar, a foot coolly propped on the sink rim in front of him.

But however Eddie is posed, his eyes must suggest that good things have been laid out on the right hand and good things have been laid out on the left hand and that he is in no danger of having to choose between them. It is the look of a host who knows that no matter which tap he draws, beer will gush forth as from an underground river. It is not insouciance, for bartending is not, to Eddie, a carefree job; his breezy expression is just the characteristic drape of his features, his slightness, the way his hair marcels up and away from his brow. In a city of panel-truck souls his is a four-door sedan with vanity plates (EW 722) and a heated garage to call home, a sedan perhaps the vehement yellow of 722 Sycamore's exterior walls. On its dash would stand a tiny crucifix.

Imagine Eddie about the time of night when Isabel and Graf drop in. Like the customers seated before him, he is framed in the backbar mirror by marble columns with ornately foliate gilt Gothic capitals, columns as white and as lightly veined as the arms of the women who are scattered around the room, smoking in sleeveless summer dresses. It is a frame that does almost everyone good, turning the surreptitious, ill-timed glances they shoot the mirror into sudden reflections of sobriety. It is a frame that would ennoble a drunken Caesar.

But this is not a crowd of Caesars. These are working Buffalonians who have cut themselves loose for the night, swathing one another in the fumes of tobacco smoke, whiskey, beer, and the sounds of jukebox music: "I Wonder, I Wander" or "Managua, Nicaragua" or Vic Damone singing "I Have But One Heart." Eddie's white shirt, sleeves rolled to the elbows, tucks into an equally white apron of coarser cotton (with industrial creases) that ends at his

knees. The apron merely lengthens his slimness. His tie
snakes smartly under the apron, and his socks set the tone
of the bar. They are fancy, the sort of abstract design one
sees on the backcloth behind a radio bandstand: curves
insinuating themselves over curves, the dull gleam of silk
woven into figures resembling longitudinal sections of
fruit.

Do what he will, Eddie seems too young to man the
bar. He floats behind the mahogany; he turns the bottles
label forward and aligns the rows of glasses in the manner
of an organist touching all the stops before he plays. His
face reveals a spread of brow his light-boned jaw can't
balance, especially when he wears a hat. His head tilts
upward naturally, or seems to do so, lifting from his shoulders. At Mass that tilted head reveals a true believer's awe,
rising to Transfiguration Church's vaulted peak, where
incense gathers in a cloud. Behind the bar the same look
stands for "What's your poison?"

What no one needs to say in Eddie's hearing is that Eddie
Wenzek, bachelor, is a catch, a deep fly ball of a Polish
son. There were early signs. His four aunts ran him in a
local baby beauty contest. He won, and stirred the wom-
en's hearts. An itinerant photographer snapped his portrait
when he was five years old; some vestige of that baby
beauty still remains. In the photo Eddie drives a buck-
board—the kind Tom Mix would take to town for fifty
pounds of cornmeal and a bolt of gingham—but his is
child-sized, "Buffalo 1925" painted on its front, and it is
drawn by a long-pronged, white-fleeced goat, whose drop-
pings dot the ground like marbles. Eddie wears an open
vest, a coarse-weave shirt with a child's large buttons, and
knickerbockers with his stockings rolled below the knees.
His curls are looser than in 1947.

As a young man of twenty, Eddie had a date—itself a
token of eligibility—with Miss Buffalo 1940, virgin prin-

cess of the Queen City, youthful emblem of commerce, industry, and transportation, her identity sunk in a geographical eponym, as often happens to women and seldom to men. (No one ever called Franklin Delano Roosevelt Mr. White House.) Miss Buffalo 1940 stood for the stately graveled paths of Delaware Park and the immortal sculpture of Forest Lawn, which had been dubbed "one of the loveliest burial places between Brooklyn and Chicago." She stood for Buffalo's numerous citizens, including her mannerly escort. She was the shallow expanse of Lake Erie, the historical thread of the Barge Canal, the world-class output of Buffalo's aniline dye industry, the storage capacity of its lakeside grain elevators, the fame of its school-furniture factories. She was the "roar and rainbow dust" of nearby Niagara Falls. She was all those things, and she looked terrific riding on the bench seat of a '37 Pontiac.

Driving home that evening, Eddie and Miss Buffalo cruised out Broadway, East Buffalo's main thoroughfare, a wide avenue of shops and large department stores, community halls and firehouses and churches. Eight cylinders ticked like a bomb under the hood. The night was soft, urbanely dark. Buildings on both sides of the street fell back before Broadway's straightness. Who knows what corridors the talk turned down as Miss Buffalo toured homeward through her demesne with Eddie dapper at the wheel beside her?

But up ahead was a wreck: a car overturned, a crowd, police in their baggy motorcycle caps and thick woolen indigo uniforms, headlights trained on the trouble at hand.

"Stop the car," said Miss Buffalo.

Eddie pulled over. She darted out her door and rushed to the crowd, pushing past the idle smokers on its fringes—a spontaneous, unofficial act, bearing beauty to the victim at the center. Sliding back into the Pontiac soon afterward, she said, disappointed, "Just a minor accident."

Miss Buffalo was an undertaker's daughter beginning to learn at home to reconstruct the faces of the damaged dead. She had done their hair for several years, giving rinses and last-minute curls to the women, making the men look barbershop fresh, so her new task was a promotion. It took more art, she told Eddie. It took experience. It took seeing bodies in every possible state of disrepair.

"Right then," said Eddie nearly fifty years later, "I got that creepy feeling."

Eddie was philosophical. "Sometimes you wine and dine a girl and instead of romancing her, you wind up at home reading the comics," he said. But wherever Eddie wandered in the neighborhood, fathers and mothers with marriageable daughters smiled upon his steps. At the King Arthur Bar, on the corner of Jefferson and Genesee, the proprietor (with a little German Princess of his own in mind) called Eddie the Polish Prince. Expectation seemed to breathe a beguine, the scent of lavender after cigars, over each chance encounter, every slim, polite flirtation.

Behind the rectory of St. John Kanty's Church, on a side street off Broadway, stands St. John Kanty's Lyceum, a brick auditorium. Under a shallow arched ceiling, a balcony lit by gallery windows circles a hardwood floor, where on odd Sunday nights during the year you might have seen a local big band at the head of the room, its brass choir popping out sixteenth-note exclamation points, its saxophone chorus pouring a sound like melted cheese over the dancers below the stage.

Imagine the scene. A man steps past the music stands to the microphone at the center of the stage, where he raises a sheet of paper to the level of his glasses, trying to find the right light. (The right light is inevitably focused on his baldness.) He begins to talk in the booming timbre of the 1947 amplified voice and points toward the sides of the room, where families and groups of friends have taken

tables for the evening—rafts of ten in a sea of milling heads.
There is applause. He points to the open bar at the rear
where the untabled gather to drink, and there is louder
applause and cheering. Someone shouts from the crowd
and everyone laughs except the band. A few last sentences,
and at the opening bars of "Rose Room" or "That's My
Desire" the floor closes with couples. Before long there
will be an interlude of Polish tunes ("How Quickly Moments Flee"), and the elders will dance too, the women
despite conflicting layers of fabric and shoes that look like
andirons, the men despite aching shoulders and the memory of how they used to move.

With music gurgling in the background like a synco-
pated fountain, Eddie passes from table to table, not a hair
turned in the comb furrows on his head. Around him there
lies a neighborhood reconstituted. Divested of the work-
week uniform (though a faint air of Mass still hangs on
their suits), men tip back on wooden folding chairs, talking
around their wives, about whom there is an attitude of
confidential display meant more for bureau mirrors than
for husbands. Their makeup is the enhancement, the illumination, of responsible modesty, the public, facial
equivalent of a thoroughly scrubbed house. The men have
dressed like dark privet hedges the better to set off the
women, who wear their best floral prints. All concede the
highest levels of ornamentation to their female children,
about whose display there is no confidentiality whatever.

"Eddie! Have a drink! You know my wife! Meet my
daughter! Meet the other daughter! Meet my niece!" one
imagines them saying. And who (but a priest) surpasses
a young bartender, the son of an old bartender, at provid-
ing the conversation required of such a moment, a man
who sees almost everyone he sees in a state of excessive
heartiness, whose very presence is—to most men and
women—like the coming of June to schoolchildren, a sign

that they can let their burdens drop like lectionaries to the ground? At each table it is ultimately dance or drink, and sometimes Eddie dances, sometimes he drinks. When he accepts a cocktail, it is with a manner which suggests that a Manhattan on the rocks turns to V-8 juice on the trip down his alimentary canal.

And when Eddie dances, it is with the flourish that comes from years of practice with his regular partner and younger sister, Florie. They dance at home in the living room of the back apartment above the bar, in downtown clubs, and aboard the *Canadiana*, a *mer douce* liner that sails nightly on a sixty-cent round trip from the Buffalo waterfront to the ballroom at Crystal Beach in southern Ontario—the most elegant and entertaining amusement park between the Welland Canal and the Niagara River. Sunday nights, the *Canadiana* carries Buffalonians on a three-hour cruise just far enough out on "the Mediterranean Sea of America" that the lights of their native city glitter mysteriously in the East while Erie divides beneath the keel.

As soon as the *Canadiana* casts off lines from its pier on Commercial Street, the slot machines begin to clatter. The rumble of the liner's dance floor (caused by engines under power) jitters up the leg as far as the knees, though it does not deter Eddie and Florie. The rumble provides a steady bass to the ten-piece Harold Austin orchestra and the vocal embellishments of Tiny Schwarz, the *Canadiana*'s singer, who sells Chevrolets during the day and stars with Dick Lecksell's orchestra at the Auf Wiedersehn. His son owns a nightspot called "The One-Eyed Cat."

Eddie is so light-boned that he makes his partners feel light-boned too, moving across the floor of St. John Kanty's Lyceum under the appreciative gaze of parents who have long since sized him up—they are patrons of 722 Sycamore Street, after all—and who do so yet again as if to remind themselves how an ordinary calf differs from a *very* nice piece of veal. They appraise Eddie for the pure pleasure of appraisal, for he reminds them that in 1947 not everything has gone to the dogs. What few flaws he has (he is not enough Polish, he has lost the tongue, but then what child is enough Polish these days, the only ones are the DPs the priests sponsor and that is not such a good thing anyway, eating lard on bread) are minor compared to his promise, which is the promise dearest to a Polish-American heart: property, filial respect, a cash business. They look at Eddie and they see, superimposed upon him like a golden aureole, the canary-colored walls of 722 Sycamore rising out of the earth just where the Polish and German neighborhoods mingle, a good corner on a major street—a bar that is not only a bar, but a nightspot with ambitions, with plans for remodeling and a change in the menu and one day a parking lot. What is now the Thomas Wenzek Restaurant will this very year pass into Eddie's hands, with plenty of room upstairs for his own family (when he chooses to marry, may it God willing be soon) and for his parents, Thomas and Freda. Eddie Wenzek dancing with one's daughter is a sight not beyond the descriptive power of a sigh.

For it is very much a case of marry Eddie, marry his world, which after all is their own world too, the world of all these levitating dancers, who one day will look back at St. John Kanty's Lyceum and wonder what it was to them, the girls who will by then have mothered girls of their own in whom is preserved the shyness they themselves abandoned two weeks after the wedding when the papal blessing wore off and they were first officially to be found "at home" with a seed in the womb and a bunch of glass grapes on the coffee table in Olean or Oswego or Cheektowaga, and the boys whose quest for understanding will have turned into fear of certain kinds of knowledge, the kinds that will be most effectively suppressed by the presence of the girls they marry, though gratitude for this will never escape the silence of their hearts.

But for now what matters is the beat, the step, the pattern that allows these dozens of pairs of bodies to constellate in rhythm. Looking down from the balcony of St. John Kanty's Lyceum, you would see that this is a society held narrowly in tension, that under the eyes of parents, aunts, uncles, godparents, clergy—adults whose relationships have crystallized—the children swing in solution, with the purposely half-held knowledge that while to collide with one's partner is a dance-floor solecism, to just miss colliding, and to repeatedly, technically just miss colliding, is romance—a means of inviting and parrying the conjugal collision that will one day be sanctioned in the eyes of this same tight society and will in turn occasion more dancing. A Sunday evening at St. John Kanty's Lyceum is an event of great concentricity.

Marry Eddie, marry his world. It is a fine summer night. As the evening ends, Eddie hears the Polish spoken on the portico of St. John Kanty's (the glottals as heavy as suet pudding, the consonants graced with an extra delectation), but to bid him goodnight its speakers switch to broad American, the tongue of Walt Disney and Al Capone, who died in retirement at Miami Beach in January, reminding everyone, as if they needed reminding, how long ago the Twenties and the Thirties were. Even the war that once seemed as though it would never end now feels astonishingly distant.

The milk-glass bulbs of the streetlamps, mounted atop shapely iron posts, cast a pavement-level shine, good for only a dozen paces before their influence fades. Neon script brightens some of the bar and restaurant windows, but most display only hand-lettered signs. The stores along Broadway are as familiar to Eddie, walking the few blocks home, as his inner voice. They are the skin of his con-

sciousness and that of his neighbors. They are buffers—
diluting privacy to a tolerable weakness—and depots of
ordinary wealth—neither so rich in wares as to seem forbidding nor so poor in stuffs as to cause alarm—the very
substance, filling all the houses round about, of a very
substantial town.

Above the smaller shops their keepers sleep. Each façade
is cut in two. The upper stories are drab: a trio or quartet
of windows set in brick or clapboard facing, curtains
drawn, a dry geranium or a ginger cat in view. Sometimes
the sound of a radio can be heard from a room suffused
with amber lamplight, a rasping cough as the dial is swept.
From time to time the gap between the buildings reveals
a shingled outer staircase leading to a rear apartment where
workboots line the welcome mat.

But the lower stories that adjoin the sidewalk are babels
of entreaty. In every shopfront, cardboard-mounted faces
smile from advertisements with purity of purpose. They
all appear to have rushed to the window to witness the
return of an amnesiac: you don't remember who these
people are, but they seem glad to see you, pipes, cigarettes,
beers, detergents held on high, eyes like portholes on a
gleaming sea, teeth the pearly gates to a kingdom where
"Candy Is Delicious Food" ("Enjoy some every day!").
The Vatican, that shop of dour saints, promises the earth-
bound far far less than these kindly cutouts do: Be Happy
—Go Lucky!

A Mail-Pouch Tobacco thermometer hangs beside a
screen door. A Buffalo *Courier-Express* rack leans against
a sill. Names and inducements appeal in all directions, as
if to levy a claim on Eddie, to threaten social distraint if a
purchase is not forthcoming: Szelagowski ("your *best* food
buy Pork Sausage"), Blue Dew, Rich's Ice Cream, O-So
Grape Drink, Wilber Farms Milk, Camels ("So Mild . . .
So Good"), Duquesne Pilsner ("Have a 'Duke'!"), Parade

Potatoes, Upper 10 Lime-Lemon Soda, Sahlen's Sausage, Wendt's Quality Chekd Ice Cream, Phoenix Imported Danish Yeast Beer, Mother's Oats, Vernor's Ginger Ale, Iroquois Beer, Sub Rosa Cigarros, Easter Brand Meats, Mary Lincoln Candies, Dr. Swett's Early American Root Beer ("Rich in Dextrose"), Coca-Cola, Cavalier Cigarettes, Par-T-Pak Beverages, Muriel Cigars, L & M Filters, King Edwards, White Owls, Philip Morris Cigarettes, Chesterfields, Kools, Simon Pure Beer, Whiz Motor Rhythm Oil Additive, White House Coffee, Sal Hepatica ("Get Rid of Constipation fast . . . when you have a Cold"), Ovaltine ("To Wake Up Gay in the Morning"), Prince Albert Tobacco ("The National Joy Smoke").

Eddie knows by heart the contents of the darkened stores he passes walking home. In any one of them, a space heater squats between the aisles, vented through a whitewashed, pressed-tin ceiling. When it rains or snows, the gray slat floor is covered with cardboard, which slowly turns to mush and is then replaced. There are low glass cases with pyramids of cans and a balance scale on top. There is cornbread mix on the meat counter, where purple sausages and wax-papered lard are for sale. On the back wall hangs a calendar from Walter Zoladz Builder's Supply and Fuel Corporation, advertising coal and coke. Wooden crates of fruit stand tipped at an angle, "Visit Mexico" printed on their sides, as though a banana floating in the morning cornflakes might turn one's thoughts Acapulco way. Near the cashbox cluster the last-second indispensables, the Hav-A-Hank Handkerchiefs and the Stick Cologne. There too hang signs denying credit or exhorting prompt payment of accounts, some simple—"BY TRUSTING WE LOSE CUSTOM"—some not—"THE DISASTERS THAT HAPPENED TO THREE OF MY DELINQUENT CUSTOMERS: ONE OF THEM SAID I WILL PAY YOU SATURDAY IF I LIVE. HE'S DEAD. ANOTHER SAID

SEE YOU TOMORROW. HE'S BLIND. STILL ANOTHER SAID I HOPE
TO PAY YOU THIS WEEK OR GO TO HELL. HE'S GONE."

On a shelf behind the counter stool where the owner
often sits there stands a porcelain Infant of Prague, like
Eddie's own, a replica of a seventeenth-century wood-and-
wax statue of the Christ Child King in Our Lady of Victory in Prague. Its cheeks are the color of eggnog. Its right
hand is lifted in a pontifical blessing. The two raised fingers
(each encircled with a gold band honoring a miraculous
cure) signify Christ's double nature; the thumb and last
two fingers touch to symbolize the Father, Son, and Holy
Ghost. In his left hand the Infant holds an aquamarine orb
with a diamond cross on top. Beneath a velvet robe, his
naked feet protrude. The robe is carefully laundered and
changed in accordance with the liturgy, a new robe purchased from the Catholic Union Store at Main and Virginia
or sewn at home from time to time. The Infant's curled
hair falls from under a lofty crown, framing the look of
ceramic phlegm it gives the customer who stops in to pick
up some smokes and a six-pack of Old Ranger Beer on
his way to play poker.

Eddie turns up a quiet block toward Sycamore Street.
His heels make sandy clicks on the sidewalk, the loudest
sound in the night except for the tree crickets, whose cries
sound like sandy clicks. After Broadway, the darkness is
palpable, an inherent property of air, as it always seems
to be in Buffalo. In place of nightfall, a dark front blows
in from the east every summer evening near nine o'clock,
drenching trees, saturating streets—especially these residential streets—with an ichor that gradually darkens and
purifies at once, till the whole city breathes and sleeps in
unison, lulled, and a lone soul out walking is likely to have
some part of his faith confirmed or denied, depending on
which direction his thoughts turn, whether they are
worked upon or not by the stillness on these porches, by

the imagining or the all too certain knowledge of the lives within.

Eddie has never lived in a private house, one without a public room where liquor is sold. What the patrons of 722 Sycamore Street like to see in a bartender is a sense of fulfillment in the pleasure they take on the premises, a conviction that the moment is just right for a shot of something soothing to the tonsils. But more, they want a rock: an outcrop which, returning day after day, they find unchanged, firmly seated, indicating true north in a landscape perplexed with false norths. They need a bartender who, when his patrons stare at their drinks as if they were altimeters unwinding too rapidly, knows how to dole out assurance simply by showing what it means to be born in a place to which you truly belong. That is Eddie, who behind the bar is a wolf in the taiga, a turtle in the pond.

But here, walking past these rows of close-set houses, which at most could quarter a side-door beauty parlor or a small-engine repair shop, Eddie is just slightly out of his element. Most of his friends and relatives live in houses like these, three times as long as they are wide. Telescopes they call them for their collapsible appearance, for the way the high-peaked, two-and-a-half-story wood-frame front gives onto a two-story addition, which is attached to a one-story kitchen, which expires in a woodshed or a toolshed, one side grown up in raspberries and rhubarb. Each addition (sometimes even the final shed) represents a generation housed within. The back apartment above the bar, which Eddie lives in with his parents, is furnished almost exactly like these houses, so there is nothing really unfamiliar in them—nothing except the ineffable loss contained in the fact that were you at 2 A.M. to wander downstairs to one of their living rooms you would not find a table of euchre going or roast-beef sandwiches set out on a steam table or a melancholy tune playing on a jukebox or an odd dozen of hatted men and powdered women crooking elbows on a long mahogany bar. Some bartenders are hospitable for money. Eddie is hospitable by instinct. He is a mixer, as his friends say. The pure privacy of these houses, were he to live in one, would threaten his nature.

Eddie turns onto Sycamore Street, a couple of blocks east of the bar. The solid run of houses is broken by corner stores and gas stations. The pavement widens to make room for the Number 6 streetcar, which runs to the City Line, where Cheektowaga starts. Eddie has lived on this street since he was two years old; the block—night or day, sun, rain, snow, hail, or glittering angels tipped from heaven—is beyond familiarity, past seeing. When change occurs, a tree removed or lampposts repainted, it provokes an apparently sourceless unease, like a mild case of motion sickness, until the cause is identified, and then at once it disappears.

This is a street of people who are thoroughly fleshed in Eddie's mind, of faces that fit, whether they drink and eat at the bar or not. These people are foundry workers and general laborers. They run radio-repair shops and liquor stores and delicatessens. They work for the railroad and the auto makers and the steel mills and the school system and the city. They jam, jelly, pickle, cook, and can. They wash, iron, sweep, callus, and blister. They are tailors and salesmen and sheet-metal workers, dentists, barbers, butchers, plasterers, roofers, and masons. They are steam-fitters. They board and they lodge boarders, some clean, some filthy. They robe and unrobe infants and Infants of Prague. They finger rosaries. They eat fish fry at the Thomas Wenzek Restaurant, or they frequent one of the other corner bars in a neighborhood where, as at every intersection on the entire East Side, two out of four corners are bars built on land once owned by breweries. When

they drink too much, they wander quietly home, their
sobriety apparently strengthened, though one or two of
them grow foul-mouthed and are forced from genteel
places like 722 Sycamore Street not by Eddie's size but by
his stubborn intensity. Their names are Chlebowy, Swi-
tula, Oleksiak, Kuzniarck, Weclowski, Zajak, Kiffman,
Augustyniak, Kuberacka, Wojtowicz, Kudlinski, Grez,
Zimmicki, Cylulski, Grimm, Hoffman, Grochowiak, Ka-
pankiewicz, Anderson, Koczur, Wolf, Skalska, Tinkham,
Naumann, Lalewicz, Siffling, Nowak, Zadrodnik, Mu-
nella, Janowski, Buczkowski, Mayer, Stephan, Isenberg,
Urbanski, Bojanowski, Ott.

And Wenzek: the name painted on the front windows
of the yellow building on the northwest corner down the
street, the one that fills its lot completely, girdled by sidewalk, leaving room for only a narrow hedge on one long
side and on the other a tiny rose garden, at this time of
night just a heavily scented shadow broken by a single
stream of light extruded from under the kitchen door. The
homes on Sycamore withdraw into their lots, but the
Thomas Wenzek Restaurant squares right up to the
traffic—a fortress, a way station, a gin mill on an asphalt
river.

There is a faint rumble overhead. Clouds have piled
invisibly into a thunderdome above Lake Erie and drifted
over Buffalo, moving like a householder inspecting a noise
in the attic with a flashlight. It is called the lake effect, the
way Erie generates Buffalo's weather, and it happens all
the time, bearing with it a stirring in the leaves as they
shed the day's dust. There is just enough menace in the
coming storm to gentle the sight of the bar, to soak it in
welcomeness. Sunny afternoons its business front looks
stark and blanched. But in this less-than-half illumination—the streetlamp devouring the shine from the open
corner door, its luster reflected on the leaded-glass lozenges

that parade above the awning—the bar becomes an allur-
ing, secretive place, the haven where Eddie imagines himself when he tells the kind of story that begins, "This
happened in winter. It was snowing like mad. You couldn't
see across the street."

When Eddie tells that kind of story, he pictures himself
standing behind the bar, socketed into his summa, his universe, the omnium-gatherum of his works and days in
Buffalo, that outpost of the Big Time. This happened in
winter. It was snowing like mad. You couldn't see across
the street. There was plenty of beer in the cellar and the
liquor storeroom was full. The world had shrunk to the
size of a barroom, which was exactly the size it always
seemed when Eddie stood there. The day outside was dim
with falling and blowing snow, and every person who
entered the Thomas Wenzek Restaurant looked around,
stamped his feet, and gave a shudder of relief. Imagine
how they would have felt if this had also been home and
if, to retreat into their beds on that snow-blanked night,
all they had to do was climb the private stairs that separate
the barroom from the dining room. That is how Eddie
feels walking up Sycamore Street with a thunderstorm
blowing in around him on an otherwise fine evening after
a dance at St. John Kanty's Lyceum in the summer of 1947.

What is more, there is a new boiler in the basement.

It came C.O.D. Graf was there to meet it. It was
lowered through the beer drop in parts and uncrated on
the basement floor. Eddie had agreed to buy the best—the
product of American Radiator, whose plant lay down by
the Buffalo River—and to buy a bigger boiler than was
strictly indicated, though not for the same reasons he
would buy a bigger car than seemed prudent. There is no
accounting, Graf said, for seasonal dips in gas pressure and
surges in demand. Eddie offered the steamfitter a Ballantine's on the house as he sat among the pieces of the boiler

in the basement, taking in the smell of sawdust and loam and damp concrete, admiring the shadows and the run of pipes in the beams and joists overhead. But Graf bought his own Ballantine's and never drank on the job. Then one day, not much later, Graf invited Eddie to throw a switch, in its small way a ceremonial occasion. The burner fired and the sound of a rising tide was heard in the pipes. It being summer, Eddie promptly shut the fire down. But when snow falls he will admire over and over the steadiness of the heat he provides his customers, even when demand peaks all over the city. Thereafter Eddie will repose in the thought of how wisely he chose, and Graf in how soundly he built.

The new boiler is only the first of the changes Eddie has planned for the Thomas Wenzek Restaurant, from which his father will retire in September. He intends to bring it up to 1947 standards, to redo the kitchen, the lighting, the menu, the mood. He wants to keep a family atmosphere at lunch, dinner, and on Sundays, but to make it feel *post-war*, less an old-fashioned workingman's bar of the sort his father created and more a fashionable late-night spot. He wants to draw a swankier crowd, a downtown crowd, people you'd find dining at the Hotel Statler or the Park Lane Restaurant and dancing at Dellwood Dances or listening to Lena Horne at the Town Casino or taking in Tex Beneke and the Glenn Miller Orchestra ("35 Ex-Service Men") with Garry Stevens and the Moonlight Serenaders at Shea's Buffalo, people who inhabit a world where the dances sound like drinks and the drinks like dances ("Merengue, mixmeister," instead of "Shot, Eddie"), the kind who know cummerbunds from cucumbers and have had their photos taken while eating at the Palmer House in Chicago and who knew just how much to tip the cigarette girl and how to smile when they looked up at the camera from their porterhouse so they wouldn't appear to be belching or nodding off under the influence of too many gin rickeys and the back attack of a greasy lunch. That is a crowd that will take some drawing.

The real work—the work the patrons will notice—starts in August, when the fixtures of the old backbar will be torn out. Eddie will oversee the installation of a new eighteen-foot backbar with a seven-foot refrigerator, a four-foot liquor display (which fits beneath the frontbar, so no bottles interrupt the beauty of the seventeen-foot marble-framed mirror, which was cut down long ago from an old mirror stored in the attic), two drawers, a cash-register recess, stainless-steel steps, a seven-foot dry storage area (for towels and aprons and napkins), a one-and-a-third-horsepower compressor and blower coil, a thirty-inch air-type beer dispenser with five lines (four beer, one water), a one-and-three-quarter-horsepower compressor and blower coil connected to the precooler in the cold room in the basement (where half-barrels of beer are stored and tapped), two seven-and-a-half-foot stainless-steel workboards, four rinse bowls, swing faucets, two mixing stations, and eight metal legs to keep the sinks and workboards upright. That, plus a gallon of bar oil to buff the sheen on the mahogany frontbar, so that when a customer sits there, she will be able to look down at that long glossy tableau and see the reflection of her cigarette burning among the beaded water rings that look like so many rises on a trout lake at twilight.

And one day soon, Eddie will add a television set, the kind he saw in New York City when he was mustered out of the service: a United States Television Projection Set, model T525L, list price $1,595. He will have a carpenter build a green leatherette console for it, raising it high in a corner of the bar where everyone can see it. When WBEN starts broadcasting in spring 1948 from the Hotel Statler, pointing a camera toward the passers-by on the street be-low because they have no other programming, Eddie will be ready. He will be ready for the customers who want to watch the test pattern over a highball.

The sky brightens, flickering momentarily like a failing fluorescent bulb. The rumbles at Eddie's back are getting sharper, more accusatory. The streetlamp at the corner of Sycamore and Herman dims and then flares. The bricks under the bar's front windows need scoring with acid to regain their natural beige. The building (again!) needs re-painting. But what it needs most of all, as a token of this transition, is a sign. Not the kind it has now, painted on the windows, but a fat and meaty sign—a tasteful bur-gundy with blue neon sidelights and stylish white lettering. It would hang out over the sidewalk, pointing kiddy-cor-ner across the intersection.

There would be no other sign like it on the whole East Side. If it were guyed to the building, it would not swing in the wind. Coming up Sycamore, you would see it from blocks away, shining at night, auguring well for the hun-gry and thirsty. If you lit it just when day faded, you would not be able to tell whether the neon was burning from within or whether the sun setting on the lake far down Sycamore Street made it glow. It would look beautiful in a late-night thunderstorm, a beacon in the driving cats and dogs. "George & Eddie's," it would read. With a post-script, "Dining and Dancing." And a codicil, "French Fried Shrimp."

The wind sounds like rain until the rain starts to fall, and then the two sound nothing alike. Eddie dashes for the front door and makes it just in time. The screendoor squeezes shut behind him. Behind the bar, framed in mar-ble, stands a man with short grizzled hair and a corporal's stripe of a mustache beneath his nose. He is Thomas Wenzek. Around him rises his particular heaven, a two-and-a-half-story canary-colored wood-frame house with a heated garage and a public bar. Above its red asphalt shingles lie the precincts of another heaven altogether, above the elm leaves and the warm rain falling through thunder.

THOMAS

The saloon keeper of a Slavic group may be the best man in it; he is at least very likely to be the most influential. It is very probably he who acts first in the matter of building a church, and perhaps piety and business combine when he secures its location on a corner opposite to his place of business.

Emily Greene Balch

There they are, the scions of Austria, in a colored penny gravure. Erzherzogin Hedwige Salvator and her sister Elisabeth Franziska Salvator wear the colors of the Virgin Mary, white with a blue sash tied over the left hip. Their mother, Erzherzogin Valerie, sits on a red-tasseled couch, which has been carried for the occasion into a glade near the Imperial Summer Palace of Schönbrunn. Behind Valerie stands her young son, a sailor's blouse beneath his blue jacket, a sailor's cap set squarely on his head. Valerie's neck is bent in maternal compassion.

In an armchair at the center of this family group sits

Kaiser Franz Josef I, Emperor of Austria and King of Hungary. Franz Josef has crossed his legs, which are neatly trousered in dark blue with a broad red stripe. He wears a robin's-egg uniform coat and a yellow belt with a sword. Rising like a battlement behind the Emperor and the women and children beside him stand six men in military dress, unhatted, mustachioed, vigilant. Their chests bristle with ribbons and medals; Prince Leopold wears a red sash.

The date of this portrait is approximately 1900. Franz Josef is seventy. Among those present there is an air of bland composure. They are a harmoniously assembled group, and yet it looks as though each figure has been placed in the composition separately and at odd angles to the rest. Prince Leopold's head is propped up by the stiff brush of a beard he wears like a third epaulet. Erzherzog Franz Ferdinand, heir presumptive to the imperial throne, stares into oblivion. Gazes wander and give nothing away. The Emperor looks forcibly at the viewer, but his expression is ambiguous. The ambiguity springs from the enormous white mustache that sweeps down from his ears and clouds his mien. Beneath it might be hidden a smile or a frown or a grimace of pain; his crinkled eyes do not say. Even in penny gravures, it is his duty to look imperial, so he wears a uniform and allows his whiskers to speak.

The only person to interrupt the ceremonial blandness of this portrait is the Emperor's brother, Ludwig Victor, whose bald, moon-bright skull mirrors the Emperor's own. Long sallow cheeks and prominent ears give him an almost clownlike appearance, but his careworn eyes suggest perspicacity or concern. He had watched—as had all of Austria-Hungary, all of Europe—the sad undoing of the Emperor's troubled marriage, which paired Franz Josef, a man who drank a single glass of Pilsener at lunch each day, with a beautiful young woman who washed her hair in egg yolks and quantities of fine French brandy. He had watched his nephew Crown Prince Rudolf stray into such vagaries—the murder of his mistress and his own suicide—that only the Emperor's prevarications could guarantee his son's besotted corpse a grave in hallowed ground. Did Ludwig Victor foresee the day when his nephew Otto, wearing only a sword, would walk into Sacher's, the famous Viennese restaurant, and salute the wife of a British peer? Did he picture Franz Ferdinand and his wife, Sophie, bleeding to death amid a forest of plumes in the back of Count Harrach's open car after it took a wrong turning at Sarajevo in June 1914? Did he foresee in that work of the Serbian assassin, Gavrilo Princip, the eventual unhinging of every premise behind the picture from which Ludwig Victor peers? Or is the look on his face just a private expression of the Habsburgs' congenital folly?

This old-fashioned gravure hangs on the upstairs, back-apartment, dining-room wall of 722 Sycamore Street. It is a more striking icon than the ceramic Sacred Heart hanging across the room or the statue of the Virgin Mary in the opposite corner. The Sacred Heart, whether or not the image itself is reverenced, burns for all Buffalonians; religion overlies their buzzing and humming like an anointed shroud. But the Emperor of Austria-Hungary surrounded by his heirs, this family gathering from the pages of the *Almanach de Gotha*, that yearbook of kings! It is an icon that suffuses the brisk American air with languor. It perfumes the room with deference. Looked at long enough, it would produce a stoop in the shoulders of many émigrés. But to Thomas Wenzek it is a last faint homage to Emperor Franz Josef I and to Austria-Hungary.

In 1906, the year Thomas Wenzek came to America, there was no Poland: there were just Prussians, Russians, and Austrians with Polish accents. Among the rulers of

Eastern Europe, Franz Josef alone refrained from attempting the brutal assimilation of his Polish-speaking subjects, many of whom lived in the province of Galicia. In the United States—sweet absolution—one is whatever one claims to be. Thomas Wenzek, born a Galician peasant, is a saloonkeeper, Democrat, euchre player, Buick-driver, and ex-Austrian who will not talk about the Old World save to remark that in such a place and in such a time he rode a cow to school.

Everyone says Tom Wenzek's shake will break your hand. Like an eel's pulse, it is his means of discharging voltage, of shocking you into acknowledging the energy he has managed to store away in sausage-sized units over the years. The handshake should not fool you. Tom Wenzek is a decent, well-liked man. The mustache—that brusque chevron under the nose, that hairy, ill-tempered circumflex—should not fool you either. It makes him look meaner than he is. Ditto the rimless glasses and the butch haircut that comes to a V at the top of his head like an arrow transfixing the man on the business end of his handshake. Never mind that he is tall. Forget the white shoes and immense arms. Looking at Tom Wenzek, you cannot imagine him a Galician peasant boy riding to school down a dusty track on the back of an undernourished cow.

Breakfast comes not particularly early—about noon—on the first day of Tom Wenzek's retirement in late September 1947. Freda Wenzek stands by the stove dicing a calf's brain she has just lifted from a pot of boiling water. In a frying pan, small cubes of bacon cut from the slab are turning black in their own grease, the way Tom likes them. Freda is a short, plump woman whose mouth turns naturally downward into the same shape as Tom's mustache. In her wedding photo, taken in 1915, that characteristic slant gives her a look of stolid patience, though she is a cheerful woman. Everything was perfect, the bridal gown, seeded and laced and pinked, the bridal bouquet a flowering bush in her hand. Thirteen siblings and friends, including Freda's four sisters and Tom's sister, Julia, had gathered for a photo staged on a Persian rug in front of Victorian *trompe l'oeil* drapery. The groom sat beside her in a dark suit, white gloves in his right hand, a white tie arching outward from a round collar, his hair oiled and mounded, the slightest touch of the bride's knuckles on his knee, the bride's eyes sighted placidly outward. And yet even though her lips were fuller then, the former Wladyslawa Freda Zaleska's mouth tipped downward at the corners. Her shoulders sloped too under the promise of a burden, as if she knew that sooner or later the honorable estate of marriage would entail hot diced brains. With the same breath that people admire Tom's handshake, they tell you that his wife is a saint. "If you wanna know the truth" is how they put it.

Freda sets before her husband a plate of bacon and calf brains scrambled in eggs, which he downs with stale rye toast and coffee. Eddie often accuses his father of eating "goofy" food. "Goofy" is synonymous with "Old World." True, Tom likes foodstuffs with a miasma. Years later, entering the apartment after his death, his children will discover the smell of Liederkranz cheese and Schmierkäse—made, as Eddie says, of everything soft and stinky Tom could find—coming from a tin plate in the pantry. Like many men his age in East Buffalo, Tom enjoys a Limburger-and-onion sandwich. Served on stiff bread at noon, a hard-boiled egg on the side, it makes for the kind of eating that rewards your attention again and again. The same is true of the homemade sausages drying on a rope behind the stove, which Tom, who takes a butcher's pleasure in handling a knife, eats in slivers shaved from the link. His jaws have grown heavy from mastication, a joy in itself, as any immigrant from his day or any DP will tell you. Dentures have scarcely slowed him down. Only one thing has changed. He no longer amuses children by lifting chairs with his teeth.

Tom stumps down the stairs with a short cigar in his mouth. He has bathed and shaved, as he always does, using a freshly stropped straight razor with a mother-of-pearl handle. Instead of a white shirt and tie he wears a Hawaiian shirt, token of nominal retirement. From behind he looks like a large and muscular tidepool. On his way out the back door, he stops and glances into the barroom. He has still not absorbed the renovations that have taken place there. Cool white and tangerine neon lights recessed in coves. Scallops over the windows. A plum-and-dark-green paint scheme. Linoleum tiles on the facing of the frontbar. A dropped acoustic tile ceiling. Venetian blinds. Artificial flowers flanking the marble columns flanking the mirror. All the bottles hidden, as if their labels weren't a bartender's private picture gallery. The place looks like the rear seat of a Packard. Eddie is not going to sell many pickled lamb's tongues in that room, even at two for fifteen cents.

For years, until just a month or so ago, black-and-white Dutch tiles marched up to the bar and formed a trough under its front edge, a long, running, irrigated cuspidor for a habit that has mostly died out. The only customer who chews tobacco in the bar any more is an old-timer with palsy. If he gets the shakes with a lipful, he has to be carried outside, drooling and spitting the whole way. No one is happy to see him, but a certain respect is owing the old-time regulars for whom this place has been as much a home as it is for Tom.

It does not even reach the surface of his thoughts, he has never had to explain this to anyone—no one has ever said, "Tom, why would a fellow want to run a saloon?" —but there is no satisfaction in the world like sitting at the front window table with a couple of friends, playing cards, smoking, drinking, watching the street with one eye, the run of tricks with the other, one ear on the gossip of old men, the other on the cash register, knowing that at any moment the door will swing open and that someone you are bound to know—someone who has married your priest's cousin's niece, someone who has drunk on the book for years and never missed settling accounts at week's end, someone busy unionizing in the ward, someone from the Twelfth Precinct, someone back in town from Cattaraugus County or Erie, Pennsylvania, someone wearing a beat fedora and just come from the river with a yellow pike wrapped in the *Courier-Express* for Freda, scales stuck to the backs of his hands—that someone will walk in with a smile showing, and even if you don't know him, he's going to sit down and order a Lang's anyway, and your very own son, the one who stayed home and didn't join the Signal Corps in 1940 and settle in New Jersey, will pour it and ring it up while you attend to what is trumps and what the current line of conversation is among these shabby but presentable old men who have anchored your thoughts for twenty-five years to date on this very corner of a great American city. Now Tom has retired to a little more euchre and a little less bartending. He has sold the business to George Ditzel (a son-in-law, married to Tom's older girl, Jean) and to Eddie. He has leased the boys the premises. They call the place "George & Eddie's," because, as Eddie says, " 'Eddie and George's' isn't phonetic."

Eddie stands in the early-afternoon light behind the front corner of the bar now, talking to Ray and Joe, the deliverymen from the William Simon Brewery, which brews Simon Pure Beer ("To be sure, drink Simon Pure") and sponsors the Simon Pure Hour of Music on WKBW. Ray and Joe are a pair in love, like most deliverymen who have worked any time together. Ray is tall and Joe is short. Ray traditionally loiters by the truck while Joe rolls half barrels down the beer drop on the Herman side of the building, where they thump onto coils of rope and old tires. Built like a half-barrel himself, Joe has a homely wife and an alcohol problem. He stays late, sometimes all night, at the brewery, drinking the free beer the company offers employees as a tax dodge. In the morning he breakfasts on a glass of sauerkraut juice and considers himself good as new, ready for another round of deliveries and a beer at every stop with his pal, Ray. (Joe will be devastated when one day Ray, the deliveryman who never strains himself, dies young of a heart attack. It is the saddest story ever heard on the route.) Joe sits with his feet tucked under a stool; Ray leans against the bar. Their heads are even. Eddie laughs at something they are saying. He has already drawn Joe a beer.

And it used to be too that on these walls were frescoes, which now lie four or five coats of paint below the surface, like a rainforest turning to coal beneath your feet. Woodlands, mountains, pond scenes in the bathroom, where Mazur, the artist, was overcome by fumes—Tom Wenzek's restaurant used to be a place where you could bring your sense of sight, as well as your palate, for a treat, for refuge from a city overblown with workaday fumes and the pallor of domesticity. It was a spot where, when your eyes slipped back into long focus after a few kümmels or three or four shots of Golden Wedding, there was a place for them to wander in the boscage on the walls or in the patterns of the pressed-tin ceiling.

This used to be a neighborhood of vigorous, if moderately chaste, sensuality, a ward and a parish that liked its sensory pleasures to smack strongly, just as it liked its religion gaudy but taut. Riotous cheeses, pungently brined lamb bleaters, coarse tobacco, smoked-liver-sausage sandwiches, corrosive blasts of spirits and solvents to wash the taste from your teeth into your gullet, birch beer on tap for children and for ladies who liked to order a Cincinnati—half birch beer, half lager—and something vivid on the walls to look at, by God, if highly-flavored German and Polish (and Austrian! and American!) visages got to be too much to take. Nineteen forty-seven comes and young people want something different: they want a bar painted all in solid hues, like some kind of plum antacid, where the only thing to look at is the way the color scheme makes the contours of your neighbor's head pop out in relief. They want satin music, music you could ice-skate on. They want a place where you watch your mouth. And Eddie and George are right for the times; the place packs them in. There is more business now than Tom has seen since 1941.

Tom's garden is just a sliver of property on the side of the bar, but he tends with care these few square yards of his former peasantry. Because he grows only roses, he tills with as much pleasure as any hard-up farmer ever took in a field nodding with barley or rye wheat. Anyone who makes the smallest gesture of interest he escorts outside to see his roses in season, then presents him with a boutonnière or her with a long-stem. This time of year, the roses are all thorn and stalk. Chalky leaves clamber up the yellow wall of the kitchen and through the mesh of the chain-link fence erected to deflect baseballs.

The sky this fine September afternoon is beginning to reclaim the depth of azure it loses when the sun is at its height in summer, though it will be overcast soon. A thin wash of horsetail clouds hangs over the west, intensifying the blue directly above. There is practically nothing to be done in the garden now, so by the shade of 722 Sycamore Street Tom begins to spade shrimp shells into the earth. (Of his new menu, Eddie says, "Shrimp were the first influx.") Tom and Eddie once loaded a borrowed pickup with manure from a Lancaster turkey farm and drove it down Broadway, feathers and turkey dust blowing behind them, to be dumped on this ever more fertile spot. Now there is a constant influx of shrimp shells, translucent gray-pink husks, malevolently odorous until the soil purifies them. Tom digs and turns and digs and turns and digs and turns. He digs and digs and turns.

◆

Impressed with their benignity, Americans assume that immigration to this country is as natural an effect as water flowing over the top of a dam. They often forget that the inducements of the United States are not the only causes of immigration. They forget to analogize, to ask themselves how hard a push it would take to make them flee their own homes. Between 1871 and 1913, a million Poles, among them Thomas Wenzek and his sister, Julia, emigrated to the United States from Austria's largest province, Galicia. (Galicia is now just one section of Poland, the name itself a Latinized version of "Halicz," the title of an old Hungarian duchy claimed by the Habsburgs in 1772.) A million Galician Poles in forty-three years does not sound like many until one considers that in 1910 Galicia's population was just over eight million and that only slightly more than half were Polish—and until one considers the sheer weight of misery it must have taken to set such a mass in motion.

Before 1919, when Poland was constituted as an autonomous republic in the aftermath of World War I, Galicia was bordered on the west by Prussian Silesia and Austria proper, on the south by the swollen Hungary of Austria-Hungary (the portion that later became Czechoslovakia), and by Russia on the north and east. Cut off from warming southerly winds by the Carpathians, the mountain range that forms its southern border, Galicia's climate was severe, but its soil was fertile. It was the kind of province that revealed itself only to natives and tended to lead foreign observers into self-made traps. The Indian subcontinent, the Levant, Africa, even the Far East, all had been familiarized to a degree, flavored with khaki and whiskey by the bureaucracies of the British Empire. Galicia was closer—over a pass in the Western Beskidy Mountains from Vienna or Budapest, across a plain from Berlin—and yet somehow more resolutely unfamiliar.

Of this province roughly half the size of New York State, the American author Francis E. Clark wrote in *Old Homes of New Americans* (1913), "For the most part, Galicia is one seemingly interminable prairie," which is exactly what Galicia did not seem to be to ex-Galicians who found themselves traversing the United States. William Bailey, writing in the *Fortnightly Review* in July 1915, found Galicia full of "the glory of snow-crowned mountain peaks, of the symphonies of the dashing cataracts, of the rushing roar of the avalanches, and the perfumes of larch and pine." Keen witness that he was, Bailey also discovered that Galicians "have a talent for sleep" and that "there are about two dogs for every person in Galicia." He concluded that "the Poles are generally regarded as the Irish of the Slav race," a sentence that tells an unwelcome truth about Austria's dominion over Galicia and hints at the decayed state of ethnic relations in Eastern Europe.

No one minces words about Galicia's economic condition at the turn of the century. In *Our Slavic Fellow Citizens* (1910), the most sympathetic of many books prompted by the flood of immigrants entering the United States in the early twentieth century, Emily Greene Balch remarked that "Nowhere else do [Poles] find themselves in so bad an economic plight as in Galicia." A year later, the United States Immigration Commission issued a report called *Emigration Conditions in Europe*, which observed that "In Galicia . . . the struggle for existence is severe." Throughout Austria-Hungary, the commission reported, "the peasant lives in a one-room hut without windows and with the earth only for a floor. The furnishings consist principally of an earthenware stove, beds, a chest, and a bench. Domestic animals wander in and out of the house at will." "In Galicia," it added, "conditions are perhaps more primitive than in other provinces."

Lion Phillimore, a traveler who toured the Carpathians about 1911, remarked of the Poles that "their only oppressor was their own will-lessness. It was a blight lying on the face of the country." In their supposed political and economic lassitude the Poles seemed to resemble one of their most important natural resources, paraffin wax, on which Galicia had a world monopoly until 1908. Paraffin has been described as a substance "characterized by chemical indifference," a quality captured in its name, which is taken "from the Latin *parum*, too little, and *affinitas*, affinity." If any region of northern Europe displayed too little affinity for the essential conditions of the coming century, Galicia was it. It had rich petroleum reserves, but they were in the hands of foreign investors, and "only 7 factories in Galicia employed more than 1,000 workers," which is to say that it had virtually no industrial development whatever.

But "great misery," as the historian Piotr Wandycz calls life in Austrian Galicia, was not simply the product of inadequate industrialization. Nor was it even the effect of the region's often inflammatory mix of widely distinct social classes and inharmonious peoples, including Poles, Ukrainians (Ruthenians, as they were called then), and Jews, as well as many less numerous minorities. Though the emperor's draft, which forbade marriage until after three years of military service, also helped provoke emigration, the critical problem—the one that drove Galicia's peasants abroad—was a growing disproportion between the people and the land.

Over the last half of the nineteenth century, Galicia had the highest birthrate in Europe, its population increasing by 109 percent. According to an 1890 census, 77 percent of Galicia's residents farmed or were somehow engaged in agriculture. "Farm" is a word that evokes a fairly precise image for many Americans, however little they may know about agriculture or the exact dimensions of an acre. A farm implies an extensive quantity of land neatly squared into fields in the midst of which sits a farmstead: a house, a barn, and several outbuildings sheltered by a grove—a dark green island in a sea of ripening corn or wheat. In the distance float other islands amid the grain, some as close as a quarter mile away perhaps, others much, much farther off. In America, a farmscape is almost always a scene of relative isolation.

To comprehend the nature of farming in Galicia, the American image of the farm must be displaced entirely. By 1910, even as emigration thinned the numbers of Galician Poles, the population density in western Galicia, where Tom and Julia Wenzek were raised, reached 300 "agriculturists" per square mile. That is an *average* of 300 agriculturists on the 640 acres in a square mile, for square mile after square mile until the land became too vertical to till. In the major farming belts of the United States, a density of less than a tenth that would be normal.

Serfdom in Galicia had been abolished in 1848, just forty years before Thomas Wenzek was born. It took nearly twenty years more to establish the peasants' privilege to subdivide the land they had come to own. Subdivide they did. As Galicia's peasant population swelled and as each family passed on to its children some parcel of land as inheritance or dowry, its arable surface grew more and more fragmented, its fields tinier and tinier. "A peasant's holding," the U.S. Immigration Commission remarked, "is not contiguous territory like an American farmer's, but is divided into strips of land often widely separated and some distance from the town." "Of all the agricultural properties in the country," Emily Greene Balch reported, "nearly 80 per cent are 'small' (that is, under 12 and 1/2 acres), and nearly half consist of less than five acres." If one had a large family—and most farmers in 1910, Catholic or not, tried to raise large families, just as they tried to raise large crops—an "agricultural property" of five acres, not all of it fertile, supported only rudimentary life. And if one's region provided neither agricultural nor industrial jobs—well, will-lessness is one consequence of chronic hunger. So is mass emigration, which is, of course, the antithesis of will-lessness.

Young Galician Poles like Tom Wenzek, who was eighteen when he arrived in 1906, entered New York Harbor with distended imaginations and the temporary, fearsome capacity—itself a kind of capital—to see the United States from scratch. When they pulled into Buffalo's Exchange Street Station on the New York Central line they were amazed to find that New York City was not the lone concentration of this country's wealth, the single apotheosis of its industrial fervor. In some ways, Buffalo was even more astonishing than New York, because here they began to learn in earnest the details of the enterprise that readily absorbed them and which they had only blinked at in New York. "Buffalo's large Polish and Italian population furnishes a plentiful supply of labor," the city told prospective manufacturers. According to industrialists, its concentration of immigrants was one of the things, like the Niagara River, that made Buffalo a logical place to develop industries that used "labor not requiring long apprenticeship or a high degree of skill."

Before they disappeared for good into the supply of

strong backs and rough hands, before they joined the factory lines and were rechristened in the name of labor, new Polish immigrants barely had time to look about them. They found themselves in a ghetto where, according to the U.S. Immigration Commission's report on conditions in East Buffalo, "the houses are without improvements; the water supply is sometimes shared by two or three households, all of which use a yard faucet; the toilets are in the yard, and in a few instances there is surface drainage." Most of the outhouses were shared by two households full of families. It was a district in which "good housekeeping should be regarded as distinctly an achievement." What relief the new immigrants felt came from finding that this was better than Galicia and that so many thousands of their kind had clustered in the streets around Broadway, Genesee, and Sycamore.

But Buffalo! Its bustle during the years of peak Polish immigration just before and after the turn of the century made anything less than braggadocio seem like sullen irony. If you came from one of the backward provinces of Austria-Hungary, where, as Henry Adams said in another context, "life is a narrow valley, and the roads run close together," it took a while to get used to the windy American notion of progress, which blew like an invigorating breeze off the Great Lakes and over the glaciated flats of Erie County. True Buffalonians, true Americans all, saw signs of advance wherever they turned their gaze. "Marked scientific progress in Buffalo," a pictorial yearbook announced the year Tom Wenzek was born in Austria-Hungary: "27 superfluous curs killed by electricity." And if you just paused to believe in it, everything around you made more sense. County Superintendents of the Poor convened downtown, as did annual meetings of the National Stove-Lining Association, the United Typothetae of America, the American Electro-Therapeutic Association, the Roentgen Ray Society of the United States, and the State Barbers' Association. Two hundred and fifty-three passenger trains a day steamed into Buffalo's five terminals. One hundred acres of the city were given over to pens full of livestock lowing, grunting, and shrieking in the awkward interval before slaughter. Grain elevators stood like capital ships on end near the harbor. The city, once a stop on the underground railroad, was progressively outspoken in its charities and services in 1906: it indexed "defective" and "backward" children, it chronicled death by overcrowding, cholera, starvation, tuberculosis, and typhoid in the foreign-born neighborhoods of East Buffalo; it authorized the Buffalo State Asylum for the Insane, the Erie County Poor House, and an Old Ladies' Home, as well as orphanages of every denomination. Over its sidewalks loomed proud Victorian buildings, the City and County Hall, the new Post Office, the German Insurance Company—architecture by men for pigeons, indubitably astonishing to former agricultural laborers who had not yet grown accustomed to working in mills and plants that dwarfed mere civic constructions.

And yet all the city's wonders—the shade of Teutonia Park; professional baseball at Offerman Stadium; balloon ascents from vacant lots; steam calliopes drawn by elephant teams through public streets; the prairie-dog colony at the Delaware Park zoo; the ornate façades of theatres and auditoriums; the seep of exquisite steams from rathskellers and restaurants, where crowds of white-clad waiters stood behind wooden chairs sturdy enough to support heavy feeding, the diners scattered under arches and braided foliage and ornamental beer-barrel butts and chandeliers shaped like castles; the race track at the International Fair Grounds and scratch racing on the avenues; *Vereins* and societies and clubs of every ilk; private and public libraries; billiard academies; Lutheran and German Baptist churches;

synagogues; great Catholic edifices like St. Stanislaus, St. Adalbert's, Transfiguration, St. Mary of Sorrows, Corpus Christi; band concerts; the roller-coaster at Carnival Court; the spectacle of erumpent patriotism at a Grand Army of the Republic encampment in Front Park, row upon row of campaign tents and a parade of Union Civil War veterans marching through a triumphal arch toward an escutcheon, a "Living Shield" of citizens at the foot of Main Street; the idle pleasure of gawking as the Erie Canal was deepened or the Hamburg Canal drained, a warlike trench with the skeletons of shallow-draft barges and the stink of prehistoric rot at its bottom; ice fishing in winter from dog-drawn, high-runnered sleds; the beauty of potted Christmas trees set out on the sidewalks in a snow-plastered city; the simple blessing of alcohol—all of Buffalo's wonders were till on the surface of a glacier of work.

By their fruits shall ye know them. This applied not only to the crowd of laborers pouring out of the East Side, "hard-faced men," as Mabel Dodge Luhan called them, men whose fruits remained anonymous, but also to their neatly individuated employers, the frozen springs of that glacier of work, the patriarchs of industrial Buffalo, men whose names were masoned into brick fronts and painted on signboards all across the city (and across the country) and for whom transcendence meant the metonymic identification of their surnames with products or product lines. By them shall ye know their fruits. Their name was legion.

They were Pratt and Lambert, makers of varnish. They were Pratt and Letchworth, makers of malleable iron and steel castings. Wood & Brooks, makers of piano ivory, piano keys, and piano actions. The Goodyear Lumber Company. L. M. Ericsson Telephone Manufacturing Company. John R. Kiem Mills, makers of pressed steel. L. & I. J. White, makers of edge tools. The George Urban Milling Company, millers and planers and shapers of lumber. Chase & Baker, makers of piano players and perforated music rolls. Wickwire Steel, pig iron. Lautz Bros., soap. Hewitt Rubber. The McKinnon Dash Company, makers of carriage and auto dashes and fenders. J. F. Schoelkopf's Sons, tanners of hemlock, and makers of hemlock, union, and oak cut soles. George L. Squier Manufacturing Company, makers of "Machinery for Sugar, Rice and Coffee Plantations." John T. Noye Manufacturing Company, equipment for milling wheat and corn. Sidney Shepard & Company, stamped tinware. Sherman S. Jewett, stoves. Hingston & Woods Dredging and Harbor Contractors. Tifft & Son, boilers and steam engines. Robert Dunbar & Son, grain elevators. Worthington Pump and Machinery Corporation. Kast Copper and Sheet Iron Company, brewers' equipment and chandeliers. Laub & Zeller, tanning. Rood & Brown, railroad car and engine wheels. Baldwin Locomotive Works. Heinz & Munschauer, refrigerators and bird cages. E. N. Cook Distillery. Culliton Ice Company. Christian Weyand Brewing Company. George Rochevot Lion Brewery. Gerhard Lang's Park Brewery. Magnus Beck Brewing Company. Schreiber's Brewery. Ziegele Brewing Company. George F. Stein Brewery. Schusler Brewery. Gilbert Klinck Brewery. William Simon Brewery.

Some patriarchs of industry took more modest trade names. Lackawanna Steel. The Buffalo Forge Company. The Buffalo Cement Company. The Buffalo Fertilizer Company. The Buffalo Pottery. The Buffalo Scale Works. The Buffalo Sash Weight Company. The Buffalo & Susquehanna Iron Company. Niagara Marble Works. The American Glucose Company. The American Radiator Company. The Buffalo & Lake Erie Traction Company. The Great Northern Railway Line and Northern Steamship Company. The Buffalo Street Railroad Company. The Buffalo East Side Railroad Company. Red Jacket Distillery. The Mohawk Brewery. The Iroquois Beverage Corporation. The Great Lakes Brewery. The Broadway Brewing Company. The Phoenix Brewery. Consumer's Brewery.

The city broke down into delivery districts gridded on top of each other, and the day divided into delivery schedules, some fixed, some flexible. No one—no one—knew them all. Buffalo ran on a vascular exchange pump, a heart diffused. Delivery was faith performed. But some days the heart failed in motive. The beat weakened just enough for doubt to creep in like an eddy in the pulse. The day fell, its weight gathered like mud on the shoes, as the laboring crowd teemed out of namesake yards and works, embarked on another delivery, lugging the carcass home to a tenement. The fume of soap was replaced on the sidewalks and in the trolleys by that of sweat and industrial leavings, by worn wools and flannels. One worked to rest. One worked to drink. Dark came, doors closed. Windows, incredibly small given the universal scale of night, spilled light onto streets darkened further by the redundant shade of elms. The smallness of the windows against the blackness would have amazed a pedestrian out emptying the dog. They were patches cut from the fabric of privacy. Behind them, within them, gravity bent bodies into grace. For the first time since early morning, flesh (not just hands) met purposefully. Laps came into use again, and loins. The workday was just a means of keeping bodies apart.

With each tick of the timeclock, the past receded, the accent softened, the English improved, and to one degree or another the mass of Polish immigrants put on America and shed the Old World, the way a person who is bound for Cleveland but runs out of money in Buffalo nonetheless succeeds in leaving Ellis Island behind him, though he never becomes *echt* Ohio. Enough changed so that when Franz Ferdinand, the tall, dour figure in the imperial family portrait hanging on Tom Wenzek's wall, was struck down with Sophie in Sarajevo, the event produced extremely muddled emotions. Enough had changed so that to young Poles once from the Austrian kingdom of Galicia the words rang strangely true when Mayor Louis P. Fuhrmann, the former abattoir boy, rose in November 1915 before the First Preparedness Meeting at the Bankers' Club in New York City, its thirty-two members gathered around a table decorated with toy soldiers marching in rank between the half-dozen oysters clustered daisy-like on every plate, and said: "Buffalo, the one uniquely cosmopolitan city of the United States—a city composed of almost equal parts of a citizenship of German, Irish, Italian, Hungarian, and Polish antecedents—is in unanimous accord with the sentiment 'America First.' "

Preparedness ended, war became a reality. "Buffalo Women Face the Hun," and indeed until 1917 many of them knew the Hun personally and thought he was a fine butcher who never gave false weight and always had such nice ground liver for dumplings. The Buffalo firm of Pierce-Arrow assembled army trucks in the Broadway Auditorium, which was normally given over to boxing bouts and meetings of the Anti-Lynching Committee, card parties for the Knights of Pythias and the Zuleika Grotto, conventions of the Arbeiter Saengerbund and the Woodmen of the World.

There were spontaneous displays of patriotism: a waterboy named Tony Monanco appeared at a recruiting center and said—his words recorded for posterity like Mayor Fuhrmann's, such is America—"Ma name Tony Monanco. In dees countra seex months. Gimme da gun." At a program to celebrate the departure of Buffalo's 74th Regiment, Mrs. Barrell sang "The Long, Long Trail." Buffalo schoolgirls formed living Red Crosses in their playgrounds; the Polish Legion reviewed Polish volunteers on the steps of City Hall; films entitled "How Life Begins" and "The End of the Road" were shown at Social Hygiene Lectures, giving the audience a clean, modern feeling, a sense that the body was at last coming into its own, that this was a war to dispel prudish cant. A replica of the United States Treasury Building was constructed in Lafayette Square for a Liberty Loan drive and later re-erected at Fillmore and Broadway, the heart of Polonia. For another drive, residents of New York State rolled a six-foot striped Liberty Ball from Buffalo all the way to Manhattan. Despite the epidemic of influenza that closed schools in Buffalo, John Philip Sousa and his Great Lakes Naval Training Station Band marched through the city, tweedling and harrumphing, warming the blood of all those who did not already lie fevered with flu. Battalions ranked in crackerjack formations swept the avenues and boulevards. A small troop drawn from Buffalo's black community paraded in a narrow column down an ordinary street. "Never before in the history of the world," said Mayor Fuhrmann of the very moment in which he spoke, "has it meant more to be an American citizen than it means to-day."

◆

On the passport he was issued in May 1929, Thomas Wenzek gave his occupation as florist. That was a nice evasion, but not an untruth. Nineteen twenty-nine was not a year in which to list saloonkeeper as your trade. In the Buffalo *City Directory*, the category "Saloon" had been replaced by "Soft Drinks," also a nice evasion. It was the federal government's belief that Prohibition hurt a saloonkeeper in the pocketbook, even though near beer was still legal. It was the saloonkeeper's belief that whether or not you were hurt in the pocketbook it made sense to appear so—

simple camouflage. Thus, to supplement the take at 722 Sycamore, which was down indeed, Tom Wenzek became a florist. In a Ford panel truck he visited growers on out-lying farms in the early morning and bought cut blooms in Buffalo's flower district on Oak Street. Freda and her four sisters kept a florist's stand at the Black Rock Market, not far from the Niagara River. Sometimes nine-year-old Eddie accompanied them. The women did business in bills only, stuffing them into their aprons. Eddie took the singles from their apron pockets, unfolded them, and counted them one by one on an adding machine. After making his flower deliveries, Tom tended bar at 722 Sycamore Street, where he served near beer as well as soft drinks with a suspicious tang supplied from tureens on the cold kitchen stove and from strangely reminiscent bottles, bootlegged from Ontario and the railyards. And on holidays, he and Freda took their place beside the right-of-way leading to St. Stanislaus Cemetery.

Along Pine Ridge Road near the gates of the Catholic cemetery in Cheektowaga, New York—a suburb that begins at the eastern city line and to which young families and retired couples and Catholic corpses leaving East Buffalo naturally migrate—there ran a long plank burdened with potted geraniums. Imagine Tom and Freda Wenzek standing behind that plank at the end of the long afternoon of Armistice Day, 1929, or rather the Sunday before the Monday that was Armistice Day that year. Like Memorial Day, this was an occasion when there were almost as many people above ground in St. Stanislaus Cemetery as there were below ground. Many remembered to bring flowers; many knew that they would find them for sale there, where rain-discolored leaves were beginning to lodge on the west side of the cypresses and to drift against the fence and against the spoked wooden wheels of Tom's panel truck.

St. Stanislaus Cemetery is an exceptionally neat burial

ground, not in the grand style of Forest Lawn, which is
filled with funereal porticoes and coffered crypts as tight
as an undertaker's smile, but in the manner of Cheektowaga homes themselves, snug two-story houses with
hipped roofs and glassed sunporches where one might keep
a cactus garden and a wicker chair. Visitors arrived at St.
Stanislaus wearing church clothes. They came at all gaits.
It was like watching new customers enter the bar: some
were easy, some not. The kind who were easiest in bars
were the kind uneasiest here; they shuffled nakedly toward
this campus of feeling, intent on preserving a good opinion
of themselves, though they themselves were not the real
object of this meditative exercise. But to many—to ladies
who held the vanilla bottle at arm's length while baking,
and whom bars disquieted—the parched soul's thirst was
slaked among these granite markers. They were the ones
who on fine June evenings sat on close lawns under sour-
cherry trees and discussed the merits of using a ground
cover like pachysandra on family graves, not because it
was easier than potted geraniums—pachysandra requires
regular care—but because it looked so much more
groomed, and grooming is a sign of life. Such people sor-
rowed over nothing more than those parts of the cemetery
where graves went untended. There the compact between
the dead and the living had been broken, and death appeared not as the interval before a lasting reunion but as
extinction itself.

The men and women who visited St. Stanislaus Cemetery on Sundays and holidays came prepared to hear
promptings from within. Usually they heard the sostenuto
of a sound digestion, vigorous seethings in a kettle of life.
But on the Sunday before Armistice Day, 1929, after the
financial buffetings of the previous few weeks, there had
been signs of distraction. It was not as bad as it would get
in a year or two, when visitors would stare at the unsettled

turf on recent graves and find themselves thinking that all wants were provided for beneath the roots in those small sod houses so trimly fit to the body's shape. But the great collapse on Wall Street—and the news, despite the crash, of a kind of phosphorescent optimism in the business and banking communities, news of the tight-vested, closely fobbed caution that Washington meant to pass for cheer —had disoriented many of the day's visitors. They had no clear idea what such developments meant, though some knew to the dollar what they'd already lost. With a start, they surfaced from their thoughts in the cemetery to find themselves moralists. It didn't necessarily help the roadside potted-geranium market. But it didn't do the bar business much harm. Bars have always been filled with moralists. Prohibition just keened their edges.

The strange look afflicting the men and women in St. Stanislaus Cemetery in November 1929 was the face of the new immigrant transposed onto that of the native-born American: the look of uncertainty. Through fear, this country's immensity was revealed to immigrants at once. The consciousness of America's size—the apparently infinite expanse of plains and mountains and marble-eyed folk lying beyond the Polish- and German-speaking limits of the parish—bore down on their neighborhoods and rounded them into incredible tightness, the way a heavy snow fused the rooftops of East Buffalo together. The men and women who drank regularly at 722 Sycamore Street could have told these troubled relatives of the dead in St. Stanislaus all they needed to know about having their feet cut out from under them. They had debated until their tongues were sour, both here and in another country, whether it was better to fear alone or to fear together, to be destitute among the destitute or merely poor among the prosperous, entirely new questions to most Americans ruined by the Crash. Even when the long-term effects of this débâcle remained to be seen, uncertainty eroded the comfortable routines, the easy assumptions. The most frightening thing about the Crash was the suspicion that this immense country (one's sense of its immensity freshened by the feeling of a nationwide loss) had become a land filled with people who had to concentrate in order to do the natural thing. People who had become immigrants in their own land.

On that dreary Sunday afternoon before Armistice Day, 1929, Tom and Freda Wenzek loaded the panel truck with unsold geraniums—knotted, arthritic plants with the musty scent of perfumed wool. They set them in flats on newspapers spread over the floor, papers headlining a New York City banker's suicide and observing that the late-October Crash could hurt only rich investors, for the small investor was wiped out in September. Tom and Freda sat for a while in the cab, where the air was still, if not warm. The horizon through the cemetery was a blur of unleaved trees broken by black vertical bands of cypress. In the atmosphere outside there was the smell of autumn verging on winter—coal, wood, and leaf smoke, and the low-flying chemical and particulate smokes from factories west and south of the cemetery. Though the truck's windows muted the sound, Tom and Freda could hear muffled churchbells down Genesee Street and the unceasing shunting of railroad cars and the whistle of switching engines in the great sidings of Sloan and East Buffalo. A few last visitors departed St. Stanislaus, car doors closing with a tin *punck*, though the afternoon was still early and the November sky had barely begun to darken. A priest walked down Pine Ridge Road, smoking a cigarette. The truck motor wheezed and caught.

Both Tom and Freda had lost fathers in the 1918 influenza. Tom's died in what was then still Austria, though the Treaty of Versailles made it Poland. Freda's father, a

Lehigh Valley Railroad hand, died in Buffalo. Desperately ill, he could not be kept from going down to the yards to pick up his last week's pay envelope. He handed it to his wife, Anastasya. Then to her and to their eight children he delivered a blessing. "You will do well and you will do well and you will do well and you will do well," he is reported to have said, encompassing them all. "But I am about to die." These words he uttered in Polish, for Anastasya never spoke anything else.

Freda did do well. She became a sister to her mother and a mother to her sisters and brothers, all younger than she. She learned to cook at the Hotel Statler. She married a man who yearned for proprietorship. Watching Buffalo's thousands of shiftworkers pour through the streets morning and evening, both Tom and Freda knew that proprietorship was the only escape from the weekly pay envelope, the only way to avoid the solemn walk that Freda's dying father took from his house on North Ogden Street to the railroad, his thoughts filled with the terrible certainty that his life's allotment of earnings had come to an end before his family could well spare them.

Tom and Freda tried a grocery and butcher shop. Tom made deliveries in a horse cart while Freda tended the counter. But there was something too static about a grocery. A grocer owns only shelves. His customers flit in and out, giving him no chance to be hospitable. His only talents are stacking and counting. But in a bar every sale is a gesture of largess, every beer a continued permission to imbibe, every whiskey an offer to extend one's leisure. A bartender may stand a steady customer a drink occasionally, and vice versa. But what can a grocer stand? A box of soap? A package of breakfast food? A container of Vermo Stomach Bitters?

When Tom bought 722 Sycamore Street in 1922 with a loan from the Simon Brewery, it was a high-ceilinged, cavernously unadorned bar, bulb-lit into dimness, all wainscoting and varnish, a bar where in the days before Prohibition a teamster with a horse van full of crated Vim bicycles ("Get There And Get Back") might pull up and soak his mustaches in lager. It was an idler's kind of place, where any excuse would draw the patrons out onto the front walk: a domestic brawl or a hailstorm or the passing of a three-horse meat wagon driven by men in kepis and white coats and laden with whole dressed hogs squinting forward on top, hindquarters of beef and whole lambs on the sides, hams hanging down in the rear, painted signs pasted all around, saying, "TALK OF THE TOWN GIGANTIC EASTER MEAT SALE/BIGGEST MONEY SAVING EVENT IN THE ENTIRE HISTORY OF BUFFALO." Nineteen twenty-two was an odd year to buy a saloon unless you had a solid faith in the human craving for sociable numbness and a conviction that this constitutional exercise called Prohibition, which could not have found a more perfect target for its fundamentalism than an Eastern European–born, German-and-Polish-speaking, sausage-eating, papist saloonkeeper, would one day expire of simple hypocrisy. The fact that in common parlance no one ever needed to say what Prohibition prohibited seemed to guarantee its failure.

Though Tom Wenzek fronted the bar at 722 Sycamore and though the very "ownness" of it, the quality that made his hold on it proprietary, legally attached it to him, the bar was really an outfolding of Freda's character. Property is a very near word to propriety; Freda united the two. She deepened her husband's natural sense of hospitality into a warmer and more sustaining welcome, a domesticity he might have found embarrassing anywhere but in a bar full of masculine appurtenances like a billiard table and a balky coal-fired stove. Her kitchen loaded the steam tables. At eight o'clock every morning, she opened the front door to neighbors on their way to work or just coming off shift.

She dealt with provisioners all the forenoon, vendors to whom Tom was almost a stranger. The geese for her goose-blood soup left behind feathers and down for the featherbeds she made for her children. Hers was the constancy Tom offended when he wasted the afternoon on a haircut that included a ritual tour of local saloons and a hangover. Hers was the decency that chastened tongues in the bar, the firmness that never needed an iron handshake or a tart little mustache to make itself felt. Hers were the sisters (and the youthful mother) whose gaiety brightened the crowd on weekends.

And when the bar was full and the steam tables needed replenishing (for in Buffalo it was illegal to operate even a near-beer saloon without serving food)—when her four children (Jean, Julian, Eddie, and Florie) were running in and out and Julie (as his parents called Julian; the "stuckee" as he liked to call himself because he was the one always stuck with chores) needed coaxing to stoke the furnace in the basement, the coal stove in the bar, and the pot-bellied stove on the upstairs landing leading to the backroom where the four children shared two double beds—when the six boarders who lived in tiny single rooms across the landing came off work and tramped upstairs and down— when the breakfast kuchen constantly needed making— when even the woman hired to help in the kitchen required careful watching, as did the porter (always a drunk) who came to clean in the morning—and when all this went on all week and abated only the slightest after a cold November day in 1929 spent at St. Stanislaus Cemetery selling geraniums to families honoring the dead of that old war to end war, the dead of that old influenza, it would not be surprising if Freda went into the small bedroom off the kitchen in the back of the building (for 722 Sycamore Street was a much smaller place then, just an ordinary house with a commercial front), sat on the edge of her bed, let the corners of her mouth down to their fullest extent, and bathed her eyes with a cold washrag. It would not be surprising. Of the old times, one of Freda's sisters once said, "We didn't need nobody else." She was right. This was plenty.

On the dresser in that bedroom sat a small black enamel box, the kind in which a woman keeps her most precious belongings and which, even as she dusts it, she is likely to pause over and turn this way and that in the light. On the lid of that box was inlaid the name "Krakowa," that is, Cracow. It was a memento of a trip from which Freda and Tom had returned just three months before, a trip to Poland in the midst of its brief incarnation as an independent republic. Tom had been tipped off by the cops that the summer of 1929 might be a good time for a saloonkeeper whose patrons were still intimate with the savors of full-bodied whiskey and strong beer—not to mention denatured alcohol thinned down to proof and aged with food coloring—to consider taking a trip abroad, leaving his home and children in the care of his mother-in-law.

For the passport photograph, Freda wore a fur stole, a pearl necklace, and a ribbed hat with a sash around it. Her chins were much in evidence. The German consulate in Buffalo issued a visa. Tom gave their foreign address as Piwniczna, his birthplace in Galicia. The couple sailed from New York and arrived in Cherbourg on June 14, 1929. They departed Cherbourg exactly two months later, having spent the night of the summer solstice in Warsaw's Polonia Palace Hotel. It was a voyage into silence, the same silence, though now that of a sovereign state, from which Tom had emigrated twenty-three years before. They returned with gifts for the family, postcard views of Paris and the Tatra Mountains, and a black enamel box with the name "Krakowa" on its lid, which is about as informative as saying that in such a place and in such a time one rode a cow to school.

But a number of things are certain about that trip. Freda felt fortunate. Tom felt rich. Freda described her children in endless, satisfying detail. Tom told his relatives about the garage behind the bar. Beside it was parked a Ford panel truck. Above the garage was a hayloft, big enough to feed a team of horses through the worst of winters. But down below, parked evenly between the posts, stood a 1925 Buick limousine, a piece of *e pluribus unum* as perfect as a bison, the sigil of Tom's naturalization. Its front fenders broke over the roadway like waves. It had mohair seats, four doors, and window shades. It was as black as the water of the Poprad River under February ice. It was the kind of car that bootleggers used, luxurious, capacious, secretive, and fast. Best of all, it only had thirteen thousand miles on it.

Never mind that after Tom and Freda returned to Buffalo in August 1929 and gifts had been presented and a round or two had been stood in the bar and Tom had caught his sister Julia up on the home news and the sighing had died down—never mind that Tom walked out to the garage, swung open its doors, and found that beneath the black lacquer of his Buick limousine, all four tires had rotted. Automotive science was still young.

JULIA

*This is a great country to which you have come.
It extends from where the snow and ice never
entirely melt on the north to where frost is never
known on the south, from an ocean on the east
3,000 miles to an ocean on the west. It has great
lakes and rivers, high mountains, fertile plains
and valleys. There are great stores of coal, ore,
and natural oil. Almost every variety of fruits and
grains is found in large quantities, and great mills
and factories manufacture everything that is necessary for comfort. This is the country to which
you have come. May you be worthy of it.*

Information for Immigrants, 1908

Thomas Wenzek's sister, Julia, was never formally ed-
ucated at all. Her parents told the school authorities in
Piwniczna, Austria (as it was then), that their daughter was
blind and kept her home to labor in the fields. When Julia
Wenzek finally arrived in the United States in 1910, four
years after Thomas, she was noticeably underweight and
had a goiter, which she attributed to overwork. It was not
Thomas who sent for her. It was her fiancé, Frank Pajonk,
a man she had met in Austria and who was now living
high on the Upper Peninsula of Michigan in a town named
for Sir Henry Bessemer, the Englishman who perfected a

means of removing impurities from molten iron during the making of steel. In Bessemer, their daughter, also called Julia, was born.

Of Frank Pajonk, there are many stories told. His mother died when he was two, his father when he was six. Frank was raised in Austria by his older brother, a musician and casual drunk. Every day while his brother was out drinking, Frank assembled his brother's clarinet and practiced secretly, teaching himself the fingerings by trial and error. Time passed, his brother drank, and Frank practiced. One day, his brother was booked to play with a local band at a wedding reception. The hour came for him to leave for the wedding, but he had not come home from his drinking nor had he carried his instrument with him. So Frank took the clarinet, walked to the wedding, and joined the band. Midway through the reception, Frank's brother burst in and found his twelve-year-old ward on the bandstand, filling the clarinet part. He had no idea the boy could play. This twelve-year-old became the man who summoned Julia Wenzek to America, where he was already working as a miner in the Gogebic Iron Range. Perhaps clarinet parables end differently in Galicia than they do in the United States.

When Thomas and Julia Wenzek were born, Piwniczna, Austria, was a town of twenty-two hundred residents on a westward bulge of the northward-flowing Poprad River, a tributary of the Dunajec, in the foothills of the Carpathians just a mile and a half from the southern border of Galicia at an altitude of 1300 feet. As the crow flies, Piwniczna lay 275 miles directly south of Warsaw, 90 miles west of what later became the Soviet Union, 220 miles east-northeast of Vienna, and 50 miles southeast of Cracow. The town hugged the river, which slid by with a steady flow, no longer a mountain stream. On Piwniczna's edges, standing shocks of grain flagged individual fields, which were broken most often by a change of ownership, but also by small woodlots or trees denoting a watercourse. Hills sheltered the town, bending its small fields into parabolic contours, tilting its upland pastures. In the southwest, the terrain sharpened steadily to where the High Tatras rose, the Poprad springing from among them, their peaks ascending to almost 9,000 feet, the dragon-toothed, granite termination of Poland's great plain and its only natural border besides the Baltic Sea.

It is always easy for foreigners to harmonize a landscape, especially one in which the signs of human culturing mingle so variously with natural forms that resist adaptation. But for farmers living near Piwniczna and all throughout the mountainous marches of Austria-Hungary in those days, this was a country of isolated valleys where beech- and fir-covered ridges no more than a few miles apart and a few hundred feet high might define one's horizons for years on end, until a stranger, one of the thousands of German steamship agents who roamed Galicia, came to visit, holding court in the local tavern, drumming the village and its outlying huts in search of prospective emigrants.

This was where George Wenzek and Katherine Dlogosz met in unknown circumstances, married, in a wholly conventional manner no doubt—a weeklong rite of wedding songs and mounted groomsmen bearing Cossack whips— and began in 1888 to raise a family of children named Thomas, John, Stanley, Julia, Mary, Anna, and Sophie. Into the mists that rain brings to the Carpathian foothills, that couple has disappeared with time, remembered two generations later in Buffalo, New York, only for sending their oldest boy to school on a cow and for telling the authorities that their oldest daughter was blind, remembered, that is, for yielding to expedients that seemed inevitable in a country where any season could be harsh, any harvest perilous, any hope scant enough to drive men and women who had always lived on the land, parceled and patchworked as it was, to make their way by rail to the North Sea ports of Bremen, Bremerhaven, and Hamburg and thus to the inner cities of industrial America, as far from the land as it is possible to go in life or in death.

Of Piwniczna, where her mother and most of her siblings still lived as she spoke, Julia Pajonk once said, "I've got nothing to go back for." But she continued to write to her family from America. She wrapped packages in cloth, stitched them shut, and shipped them abroad to a place which, though it doubtless never dimmed in her mind, came to seem deeper and deeper in the past to her, though the requests for penicillin that eventually began to issue from Piwniczna sounded up to date. It was in every respect an unequal traffic, this exchange of packages for thin airmail letters being conducted out of hundreds of thousands of Polish and Polish-American households. Many of the Poles who left Austria-Hungary for the United States saved money here, returned home, and bought more land. And many Poles, rather than emigrate from their homeland even for that long, became seasonal migrant workers in an annual pilgrimage to the orchards and vineyards and fields of Western Europe. But not Julia; not Thomas; not Frank. Those parcels of clothing and household goods sent by Julia on all their behalf were quitclaim to Piwniczna, to Austria-Hungary, to the Old World.

By return mail Julia Pajonk received a family photograph taken to honor her youngest sister, Sophie's, first communion. The date can only be guessed, but it belongs roughly to the early 1920s: George Wenzek, their father, does not appear in the group, and had probably already died from the flu. One looks and there they are, the scions of Poland in a sepia-toned photograph, their pose an unconscious, ironic imitation of the one assumed by the scions of Austria in the penny gravure that later hung on Thomas Wenzek's wall. Instead of tasseled couches and chairs, the family has gathered around a wooden bench. Instead of a summer glade with palace turrets receding beyond the greensward and above the trees, the season is winter and the backdrop is the blank wall of a roughly shingled, coarsely lapped house.

In the photograph snow obscures the footwear of everyone but Sophie, who is short enough that her legs dangle from the bench, revealing black laced boots. Wearing the white veil of a girl about to take the sacrament in the Roman Catholic Church for the first time, Sophie gives the camera a guarded look, her small mouth set firmly, her eyes unexpressive but also unmasked. The look is mirrored by that of one of her sisters (Mary?) standing directly behind her. Because Mary's head tilts slightly downward, she appears both more confident and more distrustful than Sophie. Their mother's pale visage has begun to assume its skeletal contours, exaggerated by the long black babushka falling around her neck and shoulders like a mane. Snow has clotted on her feet. Before much time passes, she and the full-cheeked daughter sitting next to her will appear to have been molded from different substances, so wizened will she become, so creviced and unyielding her weathered flesh.

In the center of the photograph there sits a man, the middle of Sophie's brothers (John?). His face is kind and exceptionally handsome, with a long, straight nose and high, elegantly graven ears. His whiskers enlarge his quiet smile, spreading it further across his face. He wears a heavy sweater with a shawl collar that rolls onto the lined lapels of his winter coat, made of thick felted wool. On his left knee he has folded his hands together—they are notable for the shortness of their fingers. He smiles honestly at the camera, and in return the camera has bestowed upon him an indescribable dignity. With the admirably serious Sophie and her missal seated beside him, he is the avatar of some principle that could not bring itself to emigrate to the New World.

Originally, there were six figures in this remarkable photograph. But someone, probably Thomas Wenzek in whose steamer trunk the picture was found, took a razor and neatly incised room between the photograph and its mount for two more. Behind his mother, Thomas inserted the bust of an image of himself taken from a photo just slightly larger than the scale of the rest of his family. The film's emulsion has lifted almost entirely away from his head, leaving behind only the characteristic mound of hair one also sees in his wedding photograph. And on the far right, against the shingled wall, Thomas inserted a full-length photograph, exactly to scale, of Julia Wenzek wearing a white short-sleeved dress with a narrow sash that ties around her waist and falls over her hip like an ornamental bell pull. She wears a locket on a short chain over a lace collar. She stares at the camera with the same setness of expression her sisters reveal, but her hair is fuller, pulled back loosely over her ears, and her eyes are rimmed with shadow. She has the mien of a person caught by the camera just as anticipation leaves her face.

Among all the artifacts families have left behind them as they passed through time, it is hard to imagine one more poignant than this photograph. Thomas Wenzek and Julia Pajonk established before their children a well-respected silence about life in Piwniczna and Austria-Hungary, though no one knows what they said to each other on the subject. But this photograph survives despite their silence. The damage of emigration has been repaired with razor cuts that make the restored, emigrant siblings look as though their feet too have grown heavy with snow outside a plain farmer's hut above a Polish river valley. And yet time has not been served. In the face of Julia Pajonk, photographed in the United States and added in her summer dress so tenderly to the picture, one can see the visibly antiquated past. But it is not visible in the faces of those three distinct persons whose hands so plainly felt the cold that winter day in Galicia. They are simply here, now. About the eyes of the three central figures—Sophie, her handsome brother, and the sister standing behind her whose bare right hand lies on her mother's shoulder—there is a directness aimed at the departed that makes the viewer feel the very presence of the present in that moment long ago just before Sophie first partook of the blood and body of her Church's bridegroom. As for Thomas Wenzek, time has eaten his Polish face away; it belongs afterward only to America.

◆

Thomas Wenzek did not bring his sister with him when he immigrated to the United States, but he did not neglect her when she arrived. She came to Buffalo first, perhaps to save money for the trip across America's Baltic to the Upper Peninsula, where Frank Pajonk awaited her in a town whose newspaper called itself the *Pick and Axe*. For a time Julia worked in Buffalo as a housemaid for a prominent dentist while her brother, still single, worked as a railroad-car inspector. She became a laundress in a polyglot laundry, her days spent in a long workroom lit by bare bulbs and animated by oversized pulleys and whirring belts, which were caged to protect hands and garments. Gangs of steam and water pipes ran up the laundry's walls and across the ceiling. A narrow walk of bare floor divided bleached wooden worktables from linen presses and ran between rows of ironing boards, wooden buckets, wicker baskets, laundry hooks, and open-grille fans trying in vain to disperse the heat that had nowhere to rise to.

Julia's co-workers were women older than she was, some with straight brown hair piled on top of their heads, others with glossy, Cyrenaic curls and stormy expressions, all attractively bare-armed, all wearing floor-length checked aprons with deep pockets, except for the mistress in charge, who dressed in a black skirt and a white blouse and who smiled in the presence of customers. Among these women Julia looked almost childlike in her quiet composure, her hair light in color as it would be all her life, pulled back from its central parting except for a few strands hanging loose about the nape of her neck and over her ears. Her eyes were dusky as always, but without the piercing, hooded quality they sometimes later wore. Whatever she was, she was not blind. As boring and difficult as her work might be, of hope, eked out by patience, there was plenty. And of formality—the natural deference, the unconscious genuflection that so ordered the humble estate of Polish peasants—there was almost none.

It was a free country, however bound one's memories might be. When the strangeness of immigration wore away it only exposed how truly foreign the United States was. Its forests and woods, though thicker and more abundant than those in the Carpathians, were somehow less ominous, as if they lacked an aura of spiritual occupancy. Its ridges were loftier yet somehow not as confining as those that darkened the waters of the Poprad River. The rhythms of life were more rapid here and far less instinctive than they were in Piwniczna, where there was a saying for every occurrence, good or evil, a sedimentary consensus that took the form of superstitions governing everything from the planting of potatoes to the disposal of a scurf of human mange.

Here labor had somehow detached itself from the forbidding sense of defeat one felt in Galicia, where even sunset could go awry, it seemed. Here the year was not an annual round of duties and rites and harvests and plantings and weanings complicated by early snows, late springs, and the turnings of ill health and scarcity. In America the calendar had been bared of all but the holiest of holy days, for time was money: here time had somewhere to go. There were Poles here who were neither Russians, Austrians, nor Germans, but Poles true and proper for the first time—at least until they began to feel more American than Polish. America is a Poland, they said to each other and in letters home: Chicago is a Poland, Detroit is a Poland, Milwaukee is a Poland, Cleveland is a Poland, Buffalo is a Poland, but a Poland of a kind that a Galician peasant tedding hay on a hillside on the happiest day of her first life could never imagine.

Here Julia married a man who spent his strength in iron mines and coal mines but who annealed himself by playing the clarinet and making violins and building bird cages from wire and wood in his spare time. Had she wed in Piwniczna, she would have moved into her husband's family dwelling or across the slope of a pasture or along the village street to a one-room hut about which she might have heard a sheaf of stories from girlhood on, a hut where the work was heavier than in her parents' house because there were fewer hands to help. There the light through the door would have made strange patterns on the whitewashed walls and on the crossbeam, and a man would have filled her bed at night. Everything would otherwise have been the same, there where sameness was the condition striven for.

But to marry Frank Pajonk, Julia Wenzek moved six thousand miles from Piwniczna to Buffalo to a shanty on the skinned earth outside Bessemer, Michigan, and then to another shanty among central Pennsylvania's coal mines, where a new sameness was being fashioned. In the foothills of the Carpathians, a national border lay only a couple of hilltops away, and as she traveled across Central Europe (the one time Julia really traveled) the people changed faster than the landscape. But immense as the United States was, its landscape always changed faster than its people. And even if the prospect of America struck her with fear, it was not the same fear she might have felt in Piwniczna. It was the difference between the fear of dissolving into an uncertain, aqueous sky and the fear of drowning in a cistern from which she had drawn water every day of her life, the path to it glazed by constant treading, its look more familiar than anything in existence except her hands, which were as worn as the stones where day after day she leaned over the cistern and disturbed its surface again.

The hardships of her early years in America Julia Pajonk never expounded upon. They were, if anything, a buffer between her and a country she had no reason to return to. What did those mild hardships, suffered on her own account in a laundry or a dentist's house, amount to compared with knowing that George and Katherine Wenzek had declared her unfit for school, confirming her peasantry, betrothing her to an unsightful tradition? They knew that the authorities, bothered by far worse problems than a case of voluntary blindness, would never question it. The authorities, those learned, influential men, would never pass a field, witness Julia working there—stooped over, addressing the furrow—and make the connection. And if they did, they would understand. This was Galicia. The earth too is blind, but how much it exacts from those who can see!

In 1922, Frank and Julia Pajonk moved finally to Buffalo, at Thomas Wenzek's invitation. There they too took up the ways of proprietorship, running the blind pig on Shanley Street, just inside Cheektowaga from the city line, that Thomas vacated when he bought the saloon at 722 Sycamore Street. The term "blind pig" arises from the old deceit of advertising the spectacle of a blind pig on view, "charging 25 cents for a sight of the pig and throwing in a gin cocktail gratuitously." Any store that sold liquor illegally became by extension a blind pig. So also were the private homes where one went for conversation with the lady of the house, who served drinks and kept a running tab on her visitors. For thirteen years, Frank and Julia Pajonk sold candy, notions, soda pop, bread, and newspapers from a modest storefront surrounded by modest houses. They sold Friday fish fry, two pieces ten cents. They sold cigarettes for a penny each. They sold pints of moonshine for half a dollar and shots for a dime. Their bootlegger was a tiny old lady who hauled liquor in a Model T. Everybody called her Van Dyke.

Seven twenty-two Sycamore Street lay three miles farther downtown than Shanley Street. It bordered a district that was predominantly German, an immigrant nationality that practically defined respectability and whose proximity marked a distinct rise in Thomas Wenzek's fortunes, an ascent from a grocery store to a blind pig to a speakeasy. That rise was the source of what Julia's children felt as the social distinction between them and Thomas's children, who seemed to live in a finer world and in a more elegant part of town.

When time came in turn for Julia and Frank Pajonk to leave the blind pig behind, they did not move downtown. They burrowed deeper into the neighborhood in which Thomas Wenzek had first settled—the Clinton Street area, just a few blocks west of Shanley Street. Just south of Clinton Street, the Buffalo River—the stream that gave the city its name and location—slumped between its banks, unnoticed, a relic of the past. It had been a century and more since the river last floated profit this far upstream, for the district from Clinton Street north to William Street and south to the river was where the railroad chose to penetrate Buffalo, putting an end to nature. It felt a long way from Sycamore Street, this neighborhood, as if more divided the two than acres of railroad tracks and switching yards.

In 1935, Frank and Julia Pajonk assumed the lease of the Black Diamond Bar, a two-and-a-half-story wood-frame building on the southwest corner of Weaver and Dingens, the railroad fringe of the Clinton Street neighborhood. It was a saloon with no extras, just a bar, a little-used back-room, capacious quarters upstairs, a garage, a woodshed, and an indoor, unplumbed outhouse connected to the woodshed. If you walked in after a day's shift you would find Frank and Julia Pajonk working slightly more than a double arm's length apart, Julia wearing a floral-print over-all apron, and Frank, far slighter than his wife, wearing a white shirt and tie. On the backbar a pyramid of bottles arose; a neat mahogany bullnose trimmed the frontbar. Frank loaded the jukebox with platters himself. Many of the songs he chose benefited from a clarinet obbligato, which he happily provided when business was slack, the notes of his accompaniment intertwining with the melody like morning glories on the rails of a disused siding.

A black diamond is of course a lump of coal. It was also the name of the Lehigh Valley Railroad's crack luxury express, a sumptuous, crushed-velvet, etched-glass pas-senger train that roared across the countryside from New York City to Buffalo, enhancing the aspirations and some-times increasing the melancholy of the men, women, and children who lived in the villages and on the farms it blew by, trailing a silence that was the richest part of its passing. Along the way, it made stops in Jersey City, Newark,

Phillipsburg, Easton, Bethlehem, Allentown, Wilkes-Barre, Towanda, Sayre, and Geneva. In Buffalo its connecting line turned north, crossed the Suspension Bridge at Niagara Falls, and headed further west across Ontario, Michigan, and Indiana until it reached Chicago. The route of the Black Diamond also linked subsidiary lines serving Philadelphia, the Lehigh Valley proper, and the towns of central New York State, among them Cortland, Elmira, Ithaca, Syracuse, and Rochester.

The significance of calling the Lehigh Valley Railroad's signature train the Black Diamond was lost on no one. In the 1930s the Lehigh Valley Railroad's freight division was the second-largest carrier of anthracite coal in the nation, ranking just behind the Reading Company. (Most of the anthracite it hauled was mined in Pennsylvania's Lehigh Valley, which lies between Allentown and Wilkes-Barre.) The significance of calling the no-extras bar at 307 Dingens Street the Black Diamond was lost on no one either. The name was all the luxury the neighborhood could afford and was at the same time a tribute to its largest employer, whose brick engine house and car shop lay just across the one-sided street, up a slight embankment, and beyond a thicket of weeds through which the feet of railroad men had cut many paths over time. If you wanted extras like crushed velvet and etched glass in the Black Diamond Bar, you chased a couple more shots of poteen with a couple more drafts.

At its peak, the Black Diamond Bar was said to serve a thousand patrons a day, a more than generous sampling of the tens of thousands of laborers who worked in all the adjacent yards of the Lehigh Valley Railroad, the Erie Railroad, the New York Central, the Delaware, Lackawanna, & Western, as well as in the shops of the Wagner Palace Car Company and other trackside industries. On their way to and from work, crews stopped in for a stirrup cup, though the stirrup now belonged to an iron horse. In that neighborhood, you might indeed see a thousand customers a day and night if you served all shifts and operated on the principle that a bar is just a room out of the rain and snow that sells liquid vademecums. The Black Diamond was more respectable but little different from the dozens of hinterland bars that annexed themselves to the railyards over the years. It was unique mainly in having a bartender—Frank Pajonk—who filled the house with canaries. "Nobody heard of parakeets those days," said one of his children, as if there were something louche and parvenu about those long-tailed birds.

During the late 1930s in East Buffalo, around the last corner down almost any street that dead-ended in railroad property, you could find a bar like the Black Diamond, virtually hidden from the street itself, its face turned toward open ground, a side door, at most, giving onto the walk. Barefoot children scratched out late-afternoon games on the packed dirt between the bar and the tracks, and they hid among the sumac undisturbed. The first time you saw a bar like this, you would wonder how the place could make a living, whether it served school breakfasts or hobo smokers or teaparties for harried wives. Its lawn was adulterated with fireweed, ailanthus, and cinders that spilled from the tracks as they rose toward a separated grade crossing in the distance. Shade trees were singed on the trackside edges. If you were driving a car and didn't know your way around, you might pull into what you thought was a driveway across from one of those bars and find yourself on the flush gravel bed of a working siding, a slow-moving switch engine bearing down on you from a block away.

Quiet as they looked, trackside bars had plenty of custom. The traffic came from across the road, from men highstepping over the rails and down the right-of-way for a drink whenever they saw fit, abruptly materializing out of a clear blue day or a dank fog or a bitter snowstorm as if the railyard were a moor only locals could safely cross. Trackside bars cashed paychecks in such numbers that they turned to the breweries for help. Some owners carried fist-sized rolls in their pockets and drove cars that seemed completely out of keeping with the district, Packards and Cadillacs. They ran tabs on the regulars until it looked as though they had taken to farming shares on a man's future. Sensible women knew to show up at the closest trackside bar a quarter hour before quitting time if their husbands weren't the kind to bring their pay home in one piece. The bartenders gave them no fuss. A man does not necessarily drink less for having satisfied a moral obligation, but he certainly drinks better.

A faint air of mystery clung to the brotherhood that patronized the Black Diamond and its kind. Reduced to a job description, their labors were simple enough, if potentially dangerous. Danger was just part of what made America's greatest open-air industry so fascinating. If you sat on a trackside porch overlooking the freightyards in East Buffalo and watched the men working almost invisibly in the distance, you could imagine their individual tasks compounding themselves into an enterprise of mathematical complexity, a conundrum overseen by a yardmaster secreted at the center of all those workers. Around him stretched an hourglass of rails, sometimes as many as twenty abreast, linked by ladders of connecting track running at an angle off the main line. To the uninitiated, the freightyard seemed, in overview, almost static, full of boxcars day after day, like a pasture crowded with blockish animals too sullen to move without prodding. But they were never the same boxcars, never the same flatcars or tankers.

Into the receiving yards, four and five an hour, came the trains, short-lived associations of rolling stock, temporary assemblies of fifty or so dark-brown cars with slightly pitched roofs and narrow catwalks down the middle, their symmetry broken here and there by flatcars and tankcars. Civilians naïvely regarded trains as elemental units snaking their length across the country, halting traffic at crossings, smoking around scenic bends that might reveal the oneness of trains even to themselves. But in the classification or shunting yard, the unity of trains was exposed as an illusion, for they were promptly cut to pieces by quick-starting yard engines pushing boxcars onto a ten-foot summit raised in the center of the yard. Under the hump lay a set of scales on which the cars were uncoupled and weighed. One shove, and gravity pulled them down the other side, where they were switched onto body tracks to await the makeup of the next train bound nearest to their final destination. Only damaged cars and switch engines remained in the yards for long. The rest, like beads on an abacus, made money when they were moving and not when they were standing still.

Outside the engine house that lay across from the Black Diamond, locomotives dumped their ashes into a huge pit. Wheeled under coal-house hoppers, they shipped new loads of fuel into their tenders from overhead. Hostlers worked on the engine fires, and oil reservoirs were replenished. The engines took on boiler water from wooden tanks. They took on sand, which engineers used to add friction on slippery tracks. If they needed repairs, locomotives were drawn into the roundhouse and parked on tracks with smokejacks installed above to keep mechanics from perishing in billows of coal smoke. Scattered outside the roundhouse lay smaller buildings—an oilhouse, a toolshed, a paint shop, a blacksmith shop, scrap bins, a lumber yard, a boiler house, an icing plant for refrigerator cars—each fed by tracks, each separated from the others by wedges of barren ground, each, from afar, completely anonymous, its function a mystery.

The freightyard at East Buffalo was as potent a cause of runaway boys (at least in imagination) as if it had been a circus wintering ground, a place where elephants lolled and clowns let their complexions clear. Some of the attractions were the same as those of the circus—the wandering life, the tight fellowship of initiates, the awe one's trade provoked in ordinary joes. Some of it was just the desire to penetrate a secret. How tempting to learn the yards—bland but forbidding by day, eerily lit by night— to be at home in what looked to most people like a threatening wasteland, to think of places like Altoona and Sayre and Renovo, railroad towns every one, as natural stopovers! But the real desire was to know the machines by which man had so dramatically leveraged his power—the Stygian locomotives or the cranes capable of lifting a derailed engine from the trench it had dug in the earth while scalding the engineer and fireman to death (the brakemen always leaped free) and turning the boxcars and caboose into tinder. That, and to explore the link between space and time which was manifestly being managed in the yards. Just across the street, the linear succession of trains running on a single track through the countryside was somehow made to overlap, to break apart, to change order while fast freights, slow freights, and passenger expresses were juggled in a manner that assured the expeditious arrival of each in cities a seaboard or a continent apart. To work in the yards at East Buffalo was to gauge the dimensions of America, which had wired itself tight with rails.

A highway is coterminous with the street and that is its limitation: it is too familiar. But a railroad track emanating from a jungle of crossovers and switches and signals and

frogs, a raised bed of ties and spikes and rails that divides
the landscape wherever it passes, that is another story: it
is discontinuous, not amenable to the automobile. You
could not watch a newly made-up train riding into the
night, its red tail lamps finally slipping below the horizon
or disappearing around a shallow curve, without feeling
the tug. If the lowest day laborer on the Lehigh Valley
Railroad crossed Dingens Street to the Black Diamond Bar
on his lunch hour and downed three ounces of rye with a
nickel bowl of Julia Pajonk's soup for company, it must
have been because he was in his glory.

The trackside fringes of East Buffalo were filled with
Poles who had been raised as farmers, people who had
once pined for mere subsistence, who could slaughter pigs
and salt cabbage and minister to an ailing milk cow. To
them an ungleaned field was an act of profligacy that threat-
ened the following year's harvest. In Austria-Hungary,
many of them had relied on the illicit good things found
in a nobleman's forest preserve to ease the harshness of
peasant life, things like firewood, mushrooms, snared rab-
bits, and game birds. In America, they turned to the railyard, itself an extensive preserve of private property.

Day and night people from the surrounding streets trick-
led across its boundary, children and babushka-wearing
women dressed in their oldest clothes, carrying bags and
baskets, wary of yard bulls and coasting boxcars. They
found coal littered everywhere among the tracks and gathered it where it lay, coal it was uneconomical for the railroads to recover. (But sometimes they removed it from
the tenders and the coal plants themselves; sometimes their
men were more felonious still and drilled through boxcar
floorboards into liquor casks. So the story is handed
down.) They gathered whatever blew out the doors of
boxcars or fell off poorly tarped flatcars—straw for their
gardens, lengths of iron and steel, miscellaneous objects of

almost any description. Near the repair shops where old cars were broken apart, they gathered wood scraps still bearing the marks of the road, boards covered with paint that shriveled and spat when they burned in the stove of the Black Diamond Bar.

On the northern edge of East Buffalo's railroad yards lay the stockyards and packing plants, Buffalo's most startling blend of luxury and chaos. From the late nineteenth century on, William Street had been edged with stockmen's hotels—the Brainard House, the Voss House, the Stock Exchange Hotel, and greatest of them all, the Crandall House, equipped with a one-third-mile track for the empirical testing of horses under wager, the first hotel in Buffalo to offer telephone and telegraph service to its patrons. Further up William, open pigpens lined the street. Extensive barns and sheds and chutes rambled southward toward the tracks, where trains packed solid with stock twenty-eight hours since its last outing were unloaded, the footing rank with manure, the hog cars dripping in hot weather from water sprayed on them to keep their delicate freight from overheating. Among the cattle and horse and hog salesmen moved the abattoir owners and their employees, as well as all the craftsmen who stiffened the stockyards against a heaving, grunting tide of livestock that could put a wooden building out of kilter just by leaning or throw a gate off its hinges or suffocate a steer or cripple a man. And among the workers moved the stock itself, driven through the parish of Precious Blood to the auction yards and thence beyond their bewilderment into the greater economy of mankind.

Their route took them through ordinary residential streets, past deep-set porches and narrow sideyards where neighbors gathered. Fights broke out between drovers and homeowners who saw their yards being trampled and their walks fouled, gutters running green and yellow and brown. Police were called in to quell riots in which stones, mud, and ignobler missiles were hurled. City ordinances were passed to confine the movement of hogs and sheep and beeves to certain restricted streets. But here too the instinct for foraging surfaced. After a procession of animals had passed by, tearing up the late morning, locals gathered "dumplings" in the streets for their gardens. At the abattoirs, in the days before a way had been found to turn them into "scores of tempting and appetizing food products," hog livers, hearts, and offal were given away to anyone who wanted them. When Thomas and Julia Wenzek were still new to Buffalo, they might have ridden down William Street on an IRC trolley lit by gas lamps and strewn with warm straw and seen a crowd of patient women strung along the tracks beside the Will Poultry Company. Every year the city markets ordered several railroad cars full of chickens for the Easter table, each car holding four thousand hens. The women were standing in line to buy the eggs the hens had laid en route to their own demise.

Where the roadway curved above the tracks funneling eastward, you could walk onto an overpass and pause at the peak of its arch, waiting perhaps for that moment when, as the bridgeful of trucks rumbled at your back and the lake wind gnawed at your ears, a freight train passed beneath you and the whole earth seemed to roar and shatter at once. On days when you needed to be convinced that somewhere some elemental vigor still thrived, the smoke and the bone-shuddering rumble would wake you from your lethargy, and you would gaze outward, refreshed by the feeling that there were mighty doings in this neighborhood.

From that overlook you could take in all of the East Buffalo yards from Dingens Street to the William Street offices of commission salesmen like Virgil Bailey, above whose door hung a sign that said, "After a good wine, a good horse!" It was a sight to instill wonder in the most cynical, that concatenation of labors, that flattened forest where men and women disburdened themselves of their animal strength. There above the glinting rails and the dull earth, beyond the dingy low buildings of the railyards and the stockyards themselves, rose the brick stacks of the steel mills and the skyline of downtown Buffalo, dominated by the nearby tower of the New York Central Terminal at Paderewski Street and Memorial Drive in the heart of Polonia, its blunted top surrounded, though not surpassed, by the twin-towered sandstone and brick churches erected by East Side Catholics as their refuge from the yards.

If you used your imagination as well as your eyes, you would be able to trace the web of connections, a network of interlinked tracks, among all those flat-roofed buildings off to the south and west. Between them lay the vast ponds, glittering in every weather, that supplied the packing plants with ice. Looming next to the ponds was the Jacob Dold Packing Company and the Crocker Fertilizer and Chemical Works, makers of Buffalo Queen City Phosphate, as well as specialty phosphates for growers of potatoes, hops, tobacco, and other crops. Nearby stood the Christian Klinck Packing Company, the New England Dressed Meat & Wool Company, and the Danahy Meat Packing Plant, the manufacturer of Easter Brand Hams, Queen City smoked meats, and Snow Flake Lard. To the southwest lay the elevators along the Buffalo River and, nearer, the Larkin Soap Company, a staggering complex which concealed in its works two immense soap kettles, each "with a capacity of 1,500,000 pounds." Between the Larkin company and the rails slipping beneath the overpass lay dozens of lesser enterprises—tanneries, harness makers, acid factories—that also flourished in propinquity to the stockyards and railroads.

If the wind let up the roar in your ears, you might almost hear a low beastly murmuring in the distance and the chattering of corrals as the herds edged nervously against them. If the shadows fell right, you might imagine an endless line of cattle and swine walking from building to building, surrendering first their corn-fattened spirits and then step by ghostlier step relinquishing their hides and muscular membranes and unguinous tissues, sowing the earth with richness made from their least parts, shoeing and sustaining and laving the men who slew them, tinting the very sun with the smoke that flew off the rendering and final dissolution of a nation of gregarious beasts. And among the shadows falling from the haze, emerging from the smoke and the dust of hooves, you might discern whole villages of people, darkly attired Galicians, moving among the kine, thumping their flanks, fingering their hides, staring into their liquid eyes, assessing with reborn awe the resources of a country that could yield such herds.

It was a view with the oneness of a train. You might go down to the ponds behind Jacob Dold's to skate or to saw ice or to drown. You might walk the tracks on William Street looking for a loose rail or a cheap egg. You might dread the crowding or revel in the closeness of the surrounding blocks. You might drift into the darkness of the railyard at night to pick coal from the tracks or to conceal from a crew boss the extent of your vagrancy. You might leave the yards bound for a respectable home or for a trackside bar where the groceries were in hock. You might do many things in this district. But you must have done them long ago because it is all gone now—the New York Central Terminal abandoned, its stairways ascending into empty space, its tiled and vaulted waiting room echoing to no footsteps, the tanneries and packing plants in its shadow now discernible only by the metallic traces they left in the soil, like the negative of an aerial photograph.

And it was already going in the Forties—the ponds filled in, the great Crandall horse barns burned to the ground—when Julia Pajonk's daughter, newly affianced to a man with a good job at American Brass, stood up to her mother and refused to have anything more to do with the Black Diamond Bar. Such is the difference between being born in Bessemer, Michigan, and being born in Piwniczna.

ARARAT

I silently contemplated the resources of nature and the feebleness of man; and when I did leave the enchanted spot, I kept saying sadly: "What! Ruins so soon!"

Alexis de Tocqueville

Corporations are immortal," says Richard Hooker the ecclesiast. They are babels in time, not space—immortal because "we were then alive in our predecessors, and they in their successors do live still." But will falters, the flesh fails, and some walls are more easily sundered than others. To a physicist—to Einstein—the "separation between past, present, and future is only an illusion, however tenacious," but the illusion's tenacity confirms, in the end, that most corporations aren't immortal at all. They're undying until they perish.

Of course, some live longer than others.

On a September day in 1825, the village of Buffalo (pop. 2,412) staged a parade to celebrate the founding of a new city to be built on four square miles of Grand Island, which breasts Niagara's stream, as one might then have put it, between Tonawanda, just north of Buffalo, and Fort Erie, in Canada. The militia, village band, local clergy, and officers of the new corporation of the city of Ararat (accompanied doubtless by dogs and small children) marched from the Courthouse to St. Paul's Episcopal Church. Cannon fired and solemn music sounded. The eye would naturally have settled upon the lone figure wearing a robe of crimson silk trimmed with ermine. He was Major Mordecai Manuel Noah, politician, journalist, playwright (*She Would Be a Soldier; or, The Battle of the Chippewa*), and "prominent Israelite" from New York City. For the occasion, Noah styled himself "Citizen of the United States of America, late Consul for the said States for the City and Kingdom of Tunis, High Sheriff of New York, Counsellor at Law, and by the grace of God, Governor and Judge of Israel." The city of Ararat—home to the Jews and their lost brethren, the Indians—was his sublime conception.

At St. Paul's, a sandstone monument inscribed in Hebrew ("Hear O Israel . . . ," Deuteronomy 6:4) and English ("Ararat, a city of Refuge for the Jews . . .") was raised to the altar and "consecrated with elaborate ceremonies." The monument had been ordered from Cleveland, and perhaps the consecration didn't take. Afterward, the crowd filed from church, only to find that the caterers and the press had erroneously gathered in Tonawanda.

That was not the worst of Ararat's setbacks. Two weeks later, Major Mordecai Noah returned to New York City for good. His sandstone monument, the nucleus of a nonexistent metropolis, was eventually carried to Grand Island and lodged in a niche, where it became a popular attraction for steamer-borne tourists. If there is a moral in Ararat, it is that whatever God may do in aid of a city, it is man's duty to alert the caterers. The press will follow.

The divine will, so elaborately summoned that day in St. Paul's Church, has done more than this for most corporations. Ararat proved exquisitely mortal, an ostentatious failure of enterprise made more embarrassing by the stately civic display that attended it. Success dignifies ceremony, and not vice versa. In every city's history, similar moments of prayer and consecration have occurred when the conclusion was no more foregone. "Hope," as Noah wrote in Micawber's vein, "is not the forerunner of certainty." Any city in its infancy might have been an Ararat, nullified at birth, stunned to discover that the effect of will is measured over time, alarmed to find that the august body of its corporation, in which many persons were chartered as one greater individual, could not sustain the breath of life even to the length of two weeks.

But the saturnine do not plan cities. That is left to optimists like Major Noah, who dispensed enthusiasm throughout his life without regard for consequences. No matter that Ararat failed. It lived during its consecration. For on that day at least, Noah—who was born to call something Ararat—had platted in his mind a spiritual metropolis rich in mythic analogies of a kind American cities commonly lack. Ararat would be the republic's Jerusalem, its official seal perhaps a dove bearing an olive branch to the ark on the mountaintop, and beneath that image perhaps the words "While the earth remaineth." What a boon for a latter-day Chamber of Commerce! How the Jaycees would love it! What a resistless fount of imagery for floats and pageants and proms! Such was the city a priori.

Most American cities were not made like that. They were not named before they were settled. They did not consciously evoke ancient myths. Time did not dim their origins nor hallow their founders; dimming and hallowing were left to orotund public organs instead. American cities were stumbled upon in the light of day—and well within range of memory—by hard-fisted settlers who knew from experience that a city is a good place to build a saloon or mark up dry goods. If you had been sanguine, you could have tracked this New World in search of a city site, catching your breath every time you saw a tongue of land at the confluence of two rivers or the indented shore of an inland sea. In America you could have founded a city and been cast in bronze. In the Old World such a thing had not been possible since the days when no one was paying attention, which was a very long time ago.

That greater individual, the city: it is a nice legal fiction and a potent metaphor, as any metaphor with humanity at its root must be. It allows a city to bestride its residents and do combat, one on one, with other fictional monads. It gives the city a more human face. It fosters paternalism of the kind expressed by Captain Willard Glazier in his book *Peculiarities of American Cities* (1885). "When the war of 1812 broke out, Buffalo was an exceedingly infant city, and did not promise well at all," Glazier wrote, as if what its citizens came to call the Queen City had been born a Dickensian orphan "unequally poised between this world and the next" and not expected to amount to much should it happen to survive.

But the little village on the Erie shore grew so fast that the trope of its humanity was soon drawn out to a nearly ludicrous extent. In "The Physiognomy of Buffalo," the annual address before the Buffalo Historical Society in January 1864, a speaker named George Washington Hosmer affirmed what all present expected him to affirm, that Buffalo had matured into a city with "a comely, noble face—open and generous, thoughtful and earnest—not grim with knotted muscles, as though born out of combat, nor soft with blandishments for the merely sensuous nature." And it was Hosmer—so alert to the phrenology of brick, stone, and timber—who depicted Buffalo's version of an arche-typal scene of American city-founding, that moment when, far from being a city, Buffalo was only a Vergilian gleam in one man's eye. "Would that a painter," Hosmer said that same night, "had been there with our Romulus of Buffalo, Mr. Joseph Ellicott, to show him to us as he rode on horseback with Mrs. James Brisbane in 1802. Through the forest trees, not far from where we are now, he pointed to the Lake and River seen through the leaves, and assured her that a great city must rise here."

The man who could write such a passage, as well as he who could utter such a phrase from the saddle, surely believed that landscape is destiny. Ellicott, the surveyor and resident agent for the Holland Land Company, which at one time owned three million acres of western New York, appeared to know almost as much about divine will as he did about the lay of his demesne, for the latter ex-pressed the former. The face of earth (another humanizing metaphor) had been shaped by God, and it was man's task to raise cities where He had been most liberal with His assets. That was the conviction implicit in Ellicott's famous parting words to the town that preferred the name Buffalo to his own choice, New Amsterdam. "God has made Buf-falo," Ellicott said, alluding to its auspicious setting, "and I must try to make Batavia."

So began in Buffalo that great refrain in American speech, the cataloguing of riches that bless one's city above all others: the rhetoric of advantages. Nobody spoke this language more fluently than Millard Fillmore, the first of two United States Presidents from Buffalo. (The second was the "buxom Buffalonian," Grover Cleveland, who retired to Princeton.) Consider, for example, a remark

Fillmore made in the New York State Assembly in 1831: "Buffalo is a point that presents many and peculiar advantages for the location of a seminary for the education of females." Perhaps he was thinking of the climate, which one writer adept at this kind of talk called "cool in summer, not severe in winter." Perhaps he meant the abundance of wealthy fathers or ambitious bachelors. It is hard to say. But he had sounded a note he would often ring, and in more robust causes than female seminaries. Opening a railroad station in Binghamton, New York, during his brief presidency (1850–1853), Fillmore was moved to misquote Thomas Gray on the advantages thus accruing to that downstate town: "The poet says, 'Full many a flower is born to blush unseen / And waste its fragrance on the desert air,' but this can no longer be said of Binghamton." That is how a President moots the moot.

Fillmore reserved the loftiest notes of this rhetoric for his hometown, whose physiognomy included an ear attuned to flattery. In the address given at his inauguration as the first president of the Buffalo Historical Society in 1862, Fillmore mused aloud: "Buffalo! Is it not a strange name for a city?" He then muddled the decorum of the evening somewhat by suggesting that "Buffalo" was a scribal misreading of the name of an Iroquois tribe once living in the area. Rightly construed, according to Fillmore, Buffalo might actually have been called Beaver, which would have left it still the only American city to bear an animal's name.

That was a rare slip from such a politic man. Usually Fillmore caught exactly the right tone, the spirit of chaste enthusiasm he used in speaking to the Buffalo Board of Trade at the opening of its new Exchange. "Buffalo," he said, "in the progress of history is destined by its position to be what Alexandria and Venice were." In that single sentence all the elements of a creed appear.

To begin with, Fillmore's statement sounds objective, a plain rendering of foreknowledge—nothing outrageous by the standards of bombast in the Victorian midcentury. Certain sentiments are likely to be broached by men embarked on great enterprises, though they sometimes sound odd after history has equivocated on the nature of progress. Buffalo—and America with it—was riding a wave in the nineteenth century; its people imagined Earth's whole ocean yearning to impel the comber on which they bobbed like preening gulls. This gave rise to a real sentiment, like romantic love, but more compatible with tight waistcoats and public parades.

George Hosmer felt it and knew that his audience would respond to its touch. "I was here in the autumn of 1835," he said, "and one morning I was at the dock, with many other strangers, gazing upon the mighty heaving western tide. There was a pile of goods and furniture all along on Joy & Webster's wharf, more than twenty feet high, and upon the top of it sat as many as a dozen Senecas, men and women; they too, with the rest of us, gazing with astonishment at this sudden flood of life sweeping over them, coming they knew not whence, and going they knew not whither."

Robert Bingham felt it too, though he wrote nearly seventy years after Hosmer. Bingham, whose *Cradle of the Queen City* was published in 1931, the year before the centennial of Buffalo's incorporation, is the sort of narrator whose favorite color is time, which he applies straight from the tube, unmixed and unthinned. He is capable of such odd locutions as "Not many years after the hand of time had passed the fiftieth year of the seventeenth century," which, once the vertigo fades, the reader is sure to acknowledge as a fine specimen of its kind. Fillmore's phrase "the progress of history" lives up to its full bathetic potential in Bingham. Describing one early voyage of exploration, he says, "Thus they passed down the Niagara River, beyond the forests matted with native grapevines and beyond the sand dunes that guarded the eastern shore, silent sentinels watching over the ground on which in less than four score years a great city would be incorporated." In Bingham's landscape, everything tilts headlong into the future, as if in a strong wind blowing from the past.

The progress of history, all agreed, was going to make Buffalo a great city, a thrumming metropolis, for, as Ellicott said, God had made Buffalo, or rather He had made what Fillmore called its "position," its natural advantages. Why did Lake Erie, one in a chain of great lakes, narrow to a point at its eastern end and make a nineteen-mile defile down the Niagara River to its famous cataract if not to bring riches to the city perched upon that shore? Why did the Buffalo River choose just that point to debouch into the lake, forming a harbor which, though inadequate as left by nature—the river outlet was shallow and sluggish like those of all Great Lakes tributaries—could nonetheless be improved by hand? Why array these advantages so profusely except to attract the western terminus of the Erie Canal?

In 1825, the year the Canal opened and Ararat was christened, a local artist named Sheldon Ball published his copperplate "View of Buffalo Harbor," the first image of the town engraved in Buffalo. A modest picture, void of hyperbole, it is a portrait of progress accomplished, not progress yet to come. Bingham's great breeze of futurity is as invisible as Hosmer's mighty heaving western tide. In the foreground stand eleven frame buildings and several sycamore stumps, their trunks gone for timber or fuel. In the background a schooner sails on Erie's flat water, while another rests at dock beside the *Superior*, a famous steam brig. At the end of the harbor squats a lighthouse and in the far distance appear Point Abino in Canada and Sturgeon

Point to the southwest, mere quavers of the artist's burin. Just visible too is the unfinished Erie Canal, which resembles a garden furrow, a place to plant turnips. There is not a person to be seen among the immensities of land, sky, and lake, not even at the docks. The whole has the effect of something Edvard Munch might have done had he worked in scrimshaw.

Yet this was the hand that to Buffalo looked like a straight flush dealt by Fate (for no one as yet knew quite how to parlay the Falls). Buffalo became, for a time, a jumping-off point, "the most eastern west," as Captain Glazier put it. The "sudden flood of life" that Hosmer saw sweeping over the dock in 1835 bore settlers from the Erie Canal to the near frontier, to Ohio, Michigan, Wisconsin, and Illinois. Flooding back in their place came lumber, grain, livestock, and ores, which Buffalo processed and transshipped, at first down the Canal and as that became outmoded along the rails that soon fretted the banks of the Buffalo River. "Supply from the West and demand from the East": that was the meaning of position.

And when the import of Niagara Falls became clear ("I wouldn't give the Americans more than ten years before they build a sawmill or a flour mill at the foot of the cataract," Tocqueville said in 1831), then it also became clear that Buffalo enjoyed a position second only to the right hand of God. G. W. G. Ferris, the inventor of the Ferris Wheel and a man, one supposes, of some imagination, spoke with laughable restraint when he said, "Buffalo will double its population within five or ten years because there the capacity of the water power is to all intents and purposes limitless." The truth was perceived to be grander than that, but it took a more visionary orator than Ferris to proclaim it. In 1844, addressing a crowd in Rochester, New York (seventy miles from Buffalo but well within reach of Niagara's influence), Daniel Webster

said, "If the Thames had a fall of two hundred and fifty
feet within the limits of London, London would not be a
town, it would be the whole world."

So London had a head start and no Niagara Falls: it
looked as though London and Buffalo would soon be neck
and neck. But to its citizens, Buffalo's future resembled
less a contest than it did the course of destiny. The phrase
Fillmore had used was "destined by its position," as if for
Buffalo track had been laid across all foreseeable time, the
underbrush cut back from the right-of-way, and the bags
checked through to the final stop.

There is no forge of rhetoric like a sense of destiny.
During the late nineteenth century, which culminated in
the Pan American Exposition of 1901, Buffalo was paved,
plastered, and roofed in rhetoric, its Victorian architecture
a perfect image of the ornaments of prideful syntax. The
very rain fell commas, snow the space between words.
Down at the dock—now channeled and dredged and lined
with rail sidings and grain elevators—you could stand and
watch the harbor pilot maneuver into port a Great Lakes
freighter, say the *Frank H. Goodyear*. Along the winding
paths of Delaware Park, laid out by Frederick Law
Olmsted, you could see tribes of children playing under
the watchful eyes of nurses—their garments dusky, cut
high on the neck—and of well-born mothers, silks and
damasks flourished about them. Stately homes receded to
the north and west, casements glimmering beneath the
porch eaves in the rose of sunset. In council chambers,
city fathers murmured in earnestness, smoke from their
cigars drifting through open windows and out over the
busy streets of Lafayette Square, where on a soapbox a
single threadbare speaker—"Whiskey," a passer-by would
think—struggled like a sibyl against the words swelling
within him.

To believe in the destiny of a city was to take literally

the metaphor of that greater individual, to imagine a communal persona that could find expression in growth and time and fate. To the 2,412 residents of the town depicted in Sheldon Ball's copperplate, the city poised at the edge of the twentieth century would have seemed the fulfillment of their proudest and most pious oratory, the sycamore stumps and eleven waterfront buildings of their village the loaves and fishes of a commercial homily. And later, when in ceremonial moments the miracle of growth needed refreshing, you could always turn back to history, where the virgin forests stood, still waiting to be warped into canal boats, and where Mr. Ellicott would always dazzle Mrs. Brisbane with his prescience. You could look back with almost parental fondness to the town of 1825 and ask complacently, Does an infant remain an infant?

"Corporations are immortal," says Hooker the ecclesiast, but whatever immortality they achieve belongs to this world, not the next. Prayers may be uttered on a city's behalf, as they were at the consecration of Ararat, but inevitably they come to sound funny after a time—like a stockbroker's orisons—for they are prayers for the wisdom of aldermen and mayors, the probity of developers and contractors, the harmony of manufacturers and unions— prayers for a decline in biliousness citywide, the success of a sewer-bond issue, the construction of a new steel mill, clear skies on the Fourth of July: prayers for a palpably human construct. A city is just enough smaller than a nation and bigger than a person to seem, as Jane Jacobs says, "wholly existential." To take literally the metaphor of the city as that greater individual, you must imagine being human under the aspect of earthly, not divine, immortality. Or the aspect of Cain rather than Abel.

Whatever the anxiety of being an artist, a parent, or a lover, there is none like that of being a city. Just when destiny seems assured—the children all tucked up in bed, the night sky cooling in autumn over the Parade and the Guaranty Building, a terra-cotta moon rising over the rail-yards and the churches and the crowded warrens of East Buffalo—something goes haywire. It may be as much as the death of a President, shot in the stomach at the Pan American Exposition by an anarchist carrying a gun with floral grips (as if he had plucked it from a bower). Or it may be as little as a nagging question: If this city looks like the destiny of the village of 1825, what will the destiny of this present Buffalo look like?

All Buffalo had ever wanted to be (and had been, since the Canal came in 1825) was hooked up, plugged in, connected to the pathways of American commerce. In 1896, when the first electrical power generated at Niagara Falls was sent down the line to Buffalo, one observer remarked, "Niagara Falls is an inexhaustible mine of wealth from which electricity will flow into Buffalo and act like warm blood running through the human body." Warm blood (like the inexhaustible mine from which it flows) is not a strong enough image for Buffalo's ambitions; it is too homeostatic. To take a metaphor from its own new age, Buffalo wanted to be a step-up transformer. Power—as trade and raw materials—would flow into the city from all directions and then, after coursing the circuitry of Buffalo's businesses and factories, it would flow out again, amplified, boosted, vitalized. A percentage of the differential would be retained as profit, and on that percentage the city would thrive, its daughters become debutantes, its sons statesmen, its corridors marble, that legitimizing stone.

But the twentieth century is a sad tale of unknotting. Trade routes shifted, shallow canals with low, fixed bridges became obsolete, the short haul grew costlier day by day, while more advantageously positioned cities rose into prominence as the country widened away from the

East. There came a moment in Buffalo's history like that
in which a precocious child realizes that precocity is over
and, what's more, that precocity has been a lifetime's
achievement. Some say that moment had always been implicit in Buffalo's rapid rise to fortune, that the city had
always known that destiny is also doom. But to its members the doom of an immortal corporation seems only
slightly less remote than the day when the setting sun will
drown in the ocean, hence the limitless reserves of official
optimism. Meanwhile, neither youth nor precocity lives
forever, a fact that is forgotten when the metaphor of that
greater individual is taken literally.

Still, nothing was really wrong in the Queen City. It
was just that by the end of the nineteenth century the
phenomenal growth of the United States had begun to
shake out the possibilities. The country had once been so
empty that emptiness itself had been a fullness of promise.
When everything to the west was almost nothing, a city
like Buffalo could be anything, even the world if Webster
was right. When nothing to the west had been anywhere,
it made sense to believe in position. Buffalo had been the
most eastern west, but that was true now only if west
meant Ohio, which it hadn't in seventy years. Now even
if Buffalo could be something different, it couldn't be
someplace else. As it matured, it faced choices, and as each
choice was made another was annulled and doubts raised.
That is what it means to be wholly existential.

In 1906, the year Thomas Wenzek immigrated to America, the Chamber of Commerce published a work called
Buffalo To-Day, intended "to illustrate a portion of the
industrial progress of Buffalo towards her inevitable destiny in the manufacturing world." *Inevitable destiny!* It
sounds doubly secure, like a state motto or the name of a
famous westbound passenger train: larger—quicker—
stronger—sooner—safer. But there is almost a plea in that

phrase, an eagerness to coax the unavoidable, a not quite Faustian unwillingness to compromise on the terms that Fate offers. Behind it one hears a troubled expectancy, almost petulance, which, to translate the mood into strictly human terms, characterizes most persons who try to repose on destiny. They find it demands vigilance and allows no rest at all. Hope is *not* the forerunner of certainty.

There soon comes a time in such a young and rapidly expanding city as Buffalo was at the turn of the century when its physical being is no longer a monument to the past or the future but merely the crux of the present. A richly articulated urban setting turns into a commonplace. Buildings cease to be intricately worked tapestries of durable matter that come afire in the sun; instead they whorl wind off the lake and into pedestrians' eyes. Names affixed to streets and parks and public spaces all over town lose their resonance, except to children, for whom they seem exotic syllables at first. New generations, new races, settle the city as if it were a primeval forest with less threat of wolves and vastly better fuel for an immolation. Manufactories (as they once were called) loom like volcanoes in a tropical peasant's field. Over time the contours of a growing industrial giant like Buffalo have all the permanence of the plaster halls at the Pan American Exposition, which were raised for the pleasures (and the political tragedy) of a single summer.

A city at that pass—one of swelling, belching, manly girth—begins to wish for an enlarged present instead of a destiny, for destiny looks less and less like the straight path to glory and more and more like the kind of chance you're forced to take when sycamore stumps still surround your town. The idea of fate surrenders to the actuary. "The way to insure the prosperity of Buffalo is to talk Buffalo all the time," citizens were told in 1901. Suddenly, prosperity was no longer an intangible promise; it was something worth insuring, like the family plate or your very own life. You might consult Bingham's hand of time, now moving rapidly round the ormolu dial of the clock of Fate, and know that Buffalo's hour was here. With possession came fear of dispossession. Before long the president of the Chamber of Commerce had this to say: "To assure Buffalo of the future growth and expansion industrially to which its advantages entitle it, we must, in the language of the business man, sell this city."

That is a painful sentence to read. It hides from its own conclusion. It borrows an argot for bad news, as if "the business man" were one of the dozen Senecas Hosmer saw sitting on Buffalo's dock, last of a tribe gone dissolute in the presence of whites and stricken by the frenzy they saw around them. And that phrase "to which its advantages entitle it": Buffalo's advantages had once been considered a gift, the object of sincere if pompous gratitude to a beneficent Deity. But now, according to the Chamber of Commerce, the "position" of which Fillmore was so proud had become the basis of a right—an entitlement to growth and unwholesome jubilation. "When a project is on hand for the building of a blast furnace," a local newspaper gloated over Buffalo's own blast furnaces, "nobody will think for a minute of Pittsburgh. That place has had its day. Making iron is a matter of geography." But the promise of Buffalo's geography had been qualified by a new realism; by 1914 the city's spirit was described, with grim hope, as "grinding away steadily and forcing Buffalo to the front to assume its rightful place as one of the largest municipalities of the New World."

Buffalo had always talked Buffalo, the way any community astonished by sudden growth will do. Men and women (and especially children) had often thought of themselves as proud citizens, flushed by reports of a sharp increase in grain tonnage handled at the docks or by the kind words of a visiting actress or by any of the other things that fatten the public ego. But it had never been so necessary to sell the city before; the city had been inescapable, "America's Gateway to and from the Great North West." If, once upon a time, you traveled on the Erie Canal, you could not miss Buffalo; it waited to embrace you, to provision you from its booming emporia for the rigors that lay ahead on the prairie farms and cactus plains of western America. And if, for nearly a century thereafter, you traveled by any of the major rail lines to the West (or to the East), the only way to avoid Buffalo was to do as Arnold Bennett did when he visited America and sleep right through the night.

To talk Buffalo in the modern age, the public needed not just rodomontade—the politician's clangor—but facts, essences of the city's achievement with which to inoculate an unsuspecting conventioneer or tourist. A zinger, for instance, along these lines, taken from an 1895 article: "There are as many miles of asphalt pavement in Buffalo as in all the cities of Europe." That fact nestles in the brain like a saprophyte feasting on dead tissue; it says, London, look out!, Paris, beware! It forces the mind toward comparisons one would ordinarily shun. Such boluses of optimism were emitted spontaneously by private citizens like A. Conger Goodyear, who called Delaware Avenue "the champion residential street in the United States." Other facts were more carefully engineered.

Of these, the best were called "Boost-a-Grams," tiny packets of cheer compiled by Buffalo's Grosvenor Library and printed in one form or another again and again. Boost-a-Grams have all the flavor and scope of postcard captions. Here is a sampling, vintage 1921: "The Buffalo Cremation Society erected the first scientifically built and fully equipped crematory on this continent." "Americanization began in Buffalo in 1908 before the word was coined."

"The Christy Minstrels which became famous all over the world started in Buffalo. They were the first negro minstrels to appear on the stage and therefore negro minstrelsy began in Buffalo." "Buffalo is the second greatest horse market and the first greatest sheep market in the country." "The City of Buffalo has at June 30, 1921, a borrowing capacity of over $40,000,000.00." "In Buffalo is located the largest plant in the United States for the manufacture of miniature automobile lamps." "Buffalo produces 75 per cent of the world's wall board." "The Albright Art Gallery has been said to be the finest building erected and used exclusively for art exhibition in the world." "The production of steel at the plant of the Lackawanna Steel Company necessitates a consumption of 150 million gallons of water per day." "Only about 20 cities in the United States have municipal zoos. Of these, Buffalo has one well up on the list, in which is the largest elephant, as far as known, in any zoological garden in the Western Hemisphere."

Facticity is clearly not the same as truth. You cannot combine Boost-a-Grams in any meaningful way, to conclude, for instance, that in 1921 Buffalonians were particularly interested in cremation, Negro minstrelsy, or wall board, or that these things expressed anything vital about Buffalo. There is no possible link between Buffalo's borrowing power and the largest elephant in the Western Hemisphere. The belief behind Boost-a-Grams seemed to be that facts, no matter how disjointed, might, if they contained a superlative, conjure faith in the city and attract new industry. If you marshaled evidence of Buffalo's stature and placed it before self-interested witnesses—businessmen, that is—they might decide that what some had called stasis and decline was no more than a readjustment of priorities. One imagines conversational interludes beginning, "Say, did you know . . . ," in which the forefinger was used as a dibble and the seed of knowledge was planted somewhere near the listener's lapel.

But this riprap of fact did not keep Buffalo's sense of destiny from eroding. You might repeat Boost-a-Grams many times before noticing how often they shouldered up to hearsay ("has been said to be") or indulged in suspicious logic ("therefore"), sketchy research ("as far as known"), and unspecified comparisons ("well up on the list"). Nor did more immodest assurances issued by industrial councils and civic organizations help, statements like "The City of Buffalo has all the favorable conditions for health, longevity and mental and physical vigor that can be desired, unequalled by any city in the United States." Boost-a-Grams were not beatitudes, though they were meant to be. Happiness was not unalterably increased by learning that Buffalo had the largest linseed-crushing plant in the United States, particularly if you had no idea what a linseed was or why it deserved crushing. The superlatives that mattered to most people were entirely different: which grocery was nearest, which saloon was most inviting, which month received the deepest drifts of snow.

"Corporations are immortal," said Hooker the ecclesiast in 1593. "The Tanning Industry is destined to go on forever," said a Buffalo flack in 1921. It is almost impossible to come of age "among the wastes of time" without seeking salvation in the continuity of species, of spirit, of intellect. It has been left to modern America to imagine it in an eternity of shoe leather.

◆

"Buffalo in the progress of history is destined by its position to be what Alexandria and Venice were." So said Millard Fillmore. In the twentieth century that statement had to be interpreted anew, for the progress of history had altered the meaning of destiny and the value of position. Suddenly, one finds at the heart of his sentence an equivalence Fillmore did not intend. Whatever glory Alexandria and Venice bring to this analogy—and both, at their very least, were places "where merchants most do congregate"—they also bring the burden of time: what Alexandria and Venice *were*. In that one word lies the dust of ages, the benison of genteel disuse, the inevitable careening of plumb lines that draws tourists like flies to decay.

But the reference to Alexandria and Venice also provides a measure of time for Fillmore's sense of destiny. What Alexandria and Venice were, they were for centuries. The United States was a new republic—all its towns fresh from the ground up—but who would have guessed that any of them would have such short expectations? Who would imagine that little more than a century would suffice to carry one from Mr. Ellicott gesturing on horseback toward the spot where a great city must arise to the president of the Chamber of Commerce announcing that in the parlance of his membership that same city must be flogged like a new brand of soap? Time was supposed to allow a melismatic flourish over each of a city's days, the tempering of colors into a harmony that could not exist unless half a millennium of weather had done its work. Whatever time was for, it was not for such swift conveyance of adversity.

Given the whole of the Christian era in which to develop, a city might find means to cope with decline. For consolation it might appeal to the example of Rome, sacked; of Carthage, annihilated; of Babylon, outmoded; of Jerusalem, dispersed; of Ararat, stillborn. It might cultivate its garden, or rejoice that in the fullness of time there is room to rise and fall and rise again. It might reflect upon the possibility that a city has no destiny except as a record of done deeds—that its task is to allow its residents to nourish themselves in mind and body, while to have done that well is destiny enough. It might listen with a mordant smile to the pratings of its most ambitious champions. It might grow ancient and wise.

But it may be that the nineteenth century was a bad time to become a city, the rhetorical diet too rich, the stakes too high for rational ambitions. Every American city, new or not, sensed the latent force of the nation in the nineteenth century and wanted nothing more than to be the conduit through which it spent itself in the twentieth, whatever the cost in local delirium. "Man," said Henry Adams, speaking of the twentieth century, "had translated himself into a new universe which had no common scale of measurement with the old"; and that included the scale of time. There was Old World time, and there was New World time: expectations, not clocks, were adjusted when passing from one to the other. In America a city might rise from forest into a smoking red brick Gehenna in less than a century (and be called "great" by politicians and historians). But what would be its resources—the depth of its philosophy if its only philosophy was growth—when at first it started to fail to grow and then began to decline? It would be one thing if a city, once built, could be unbuilt for profit according to its needs, bricks restored to their hods, asphalt lifted and the sod regreened. But that economy only the organic world affords.

In decline, Buffalo's refuge was stoic pride, which climaxed at its Centennial. For ten days in early July 1932, in the depths of the Depression, Buffalo staged a Neronian celebration, the rooftops set aflame with grandiloquence. The Centennial was a Boost-a-Gram come to life, a review, in the words of Mayor Charles Roesch, "of inspiring accomplishment in the fields of civic, commercial, and cultural endeavor [which] will bring to every citizen and every visitor an equally inspiring faith in the future of our great city." Day after day, aerialists tumbled through the atmosphere; horseshoes were tossed in tournaments; massed children marched; and massed choirs sang "majestic National Hymns" with massed bands accompanying them. Night after night the festivities ended in fireworks, which were grand, massive, spectacular, mammoth, or tremendous, depending on the date. The world première and only performance of the "Music Drama 'Deliverance' " (the story of Joseph) was enacted with "a great chorus of 1000 voices, [and] many hundreds of costumed people on the stage," while at 4 P.M. on the Fourth of July a "fleet of airplanes flying in war formation" bombed the city. Had the thought occurred, Cleopatra would have sailed the Erie Canal on her barge, its "strange invisible perfume" pickling the air in honor of Fillmore's Alexandrian allusion.

The climax of pride and hyperbole came in two pageants written just for the Centennial. The first was "The Romance of Buffalo" by Josephine Wilhelm Wickser, which told in three parts (twenty-seven episodes of municipal verse) the saga of the city from prehistory onward ("'Tis fitting that men pause today and hear/ The story of Niagara's Frontier, / For Buffalo's superb inheritance / Came from the ages—not through merest chance!"). And on Sunday, July 10, the final night of festivity, the students of Canisius College and Alice V. Munger's School of Dancing presented a "Masque of Civilization" written by the Reverend Edward B. Bunn, S.J. Dramatizing "the conflict of human forces involved in the making of a great city," the masque portrayed "Buffalo's betrothal to Civilization" as well as that consummate moment when—after "Education, Industry, Transportation, Newspapers, Art and Science make phenomenal progress"—"Buffalo reaches the stature of mature womanhood whom Civilization chooses as his queen." (This was the same queen of whom it had recently been said, "Buffalo has 3,000 manufacturers now . . . and she wants more.") The masque concluded with the "Banishment of Barbarism" and a "Dance of the Muses." As Centennial Park emptied out that night, there no doubt hung in the air a musk caused by the widespread arousal of civic emotions, as if fatigues from an antique war had been brought out and beaten in moonlight till their dust had choked the eyes.

With that, the city fell back spent.

◆

And yet. And yet.

After such rhetoric, what ruin? After all the trumpeting of destiny, you would think that Buffalo in decline (no longer the eighth city in the nation) must have turned sepulchral out of shame. You'd imagine a scene straight from Gibbon: the mayor in weeds, expressing "serene confidence" in Buffalo's future (the serenity of St. Sebastian as the arrows found their mark), while marble spalled from monuments and down an alley on one wretched dawn a drunken rhetor stumbled on the carcass of a lion. If there was a ghostly presence in that urban relict, it was the echo of its oratory coming back to haunt it.

But if a city can't be London, Alexandria, or Venice, what harm is there in being Buffalo? Just Buffalo, as one might learn to say, an ordinary city of half a million souls or less. The Lake had not been moved; the Falls had not been shortened.

Imagine you are a brisk, abbreviated beauty like Renee Celline, whom Eddie Wenzek will marry one day, moving to Buffalo from Renovo, Pennsylvania. The year is 1947. Renee is the kind of girl who ran barefoot in the hills along the Susquehanna River with her brothers. She wrote her name on walls with sticks dipped in the tar of sun-softened streets. As a child she rode the trains shunting in and out of the Renovo yards, where her father, Carmen, worked. for the Pennsylvania Railroad and was a member of the Brotherhood of Locomotive Firemen and Engineers. At home he gardened and made cherry wine. Sometimes Renee stood with her mother, Jennie, at the end of the footbridge that crossed the tracks from the yards into East Renovo, and there she discovered that, unlike most of the men she saw walking toward her, her father, who worked in the engine house and so had a personal locker, came home clean from his work. She resolved to marry a clean man. Eddie Wenzek was waiting.

When war came, Renee oiled the lubricators on locomotives in the Williamsport yards. She enlisted in the WAVES and traveled by rail to San Francisco, where she embarked for Pearl Harbor. In Hawaii, she rose to the rank of Petty Officer Second Class and the rating of Storekeeper Second Class. She fought the war with a clipboard in hand, checking, disbursing, receipting. She came to Buffalo with a girlfriend after the dislodgings of the war, at a time when to return from the service and marry and bear children and age and bury your husband and die while wearing an apron in the middle of nowhere had begun to look stale to her. She had lived in barracks and aboard a ship, but had never really settled in a city, never really put off the small town.

Say you're Renee, someone for whom the Queen City is decidedly somewhere. Everything seems new from the window of your girlfriend's father's car rolling through the countryside toward Buffalo, a place where who knows how they make their money and who knows what it buys. Fields tumble down to narrow washes where the brush grows thick; smoke rises in a curtain from behind a hill and tints the light. You ride past old brick silos, weathered hayricks, wetland thatch, a shuttered roadhouse, rutted tracks that wander off the highway into clover, through settled crossroads, over hilltops, until soon the hilltop is unbroken, no hollow left at all, the landscape squaring for a view. It makes you sit right up and tap your foot against the floorboard, as if a sound track were beginning to be heard—"Tuxedo Junction," you would swear—from where the city's lights would be if it were dark.

Then comes a single house connected not to country but to city. The house is waiting there for houses that haven't yet arrived. (The land on which it sits leads to the house, while on a farm the house leads to the land on which it sits.) The telephone poles that run along the ditch add one arm, then another and another above the hydrants that begin to pop up. A railroad track swings tandem to the road, then another and another until sidings glisten off toward the near horizon. The temper of the landscape changes utterly. On every street you pass, the setback shrinks until the sidewalk disappears. You soon come eye to eye with stone foundations, loading docks, and iron doors that set off klaxons when they open, private highways, private railroads, private cataclysms, whole townships of ground entombed in brick. Everywhere there are danger, caution, warning—no thoroughfare, no exit, no admittance. They could duplicate down here the fate of Lot's unlistening wife or administer Nebuchadnezzar's justice. Walkways cantilever into wooden sheds atop the highest structures, grated loopholes ventilate alleys of blank brick walls, ladders climb the sides of tanks from which flow conduits that arch across the road and vanish into lattices of valves and pumps and Y-joints. And no one in sight, though there are signs of humans: a coffee cup set on a window sill, a fire door propped open with a broom, the starting of a single diesel engine in a yard of silent trucks.

Here nothing is for sale that anyone would buy who did not already know how all this territory worked. Orders would arrive in tankcars, the bellies stenciled with codes.

The buyer would sign an invoice for the purchase of some fifty thousand gallons of a substance which when mixed with several other substances in pond-sized vats he happened to have handy would yield a substance that would coat a metal to prepare it for a process it would one day undergo before a factory turned it into something that someone like you had never seen. In one brief turning you are on a drawbridge above the Buffalo River, tires humming on the roadway's steel reticulum. This is a river in which sinuousness—any tendency to eel along—has been cured; it flows from corner to corner in a straight line, or rather it pools in neatly jointed quadrates, transecting canals and basins of equal angularity. The car turns up a side street where the river laps against a breast wall. Across the channel, a ship offloads near a bank of concrete grain elevators. The water in the shadow of the freighter's stern is colored rust and gray. Each wavelet curls against the hull like a weak adhesive. You wonder whether, instead of water, they use within these slips some technical shipfloating fluid made in giant cauldrons in another part of town.

The buildings grow in scale, their billows reaching higher in the fug, and then it dawns on you (who thought you knew your father's utmost labors) that all these bricks—these miles and miles and miles of layered courses interlocked and mortared into gables, ledges, smokestacks, walls, and window arches, filigrees of ornament where in the mason's highly structured jazz a brick is turned or set up vertically or sloped into a herringbone, each brick a variation on the character of umber, now black, now almost orange—it dawns on you that all these bricks were laid by hand. It dizzies, for it opens up a nearly infinite regression. The bricks were laid by hand and manufactured by machine, but how were the machines made? And who made the machines that made the matter from which machines were made? And then who manufactured those machines? If you push the question far enough, you come at last upon a solitary figure sitting on a beach at night and pounding rocks together in a driftwood fire. The farther down these streets you go, the nearer seems some fundamental moment, some elemental scene, the place where steel dissolves into its raw materials. You glimpse a city built of furnaces whose stoking is the work of railway-mounted gantries, booms, and hoppers, its fuel heaped in mounds beside them. The plants along the lakefront bear witness to the human capacity to contain fear.

More streets, more factories, more turnings toward the north, a faintly residential neighborhood. Soon come homes and bars and car barns, low-hung structures. Then the railroad shears away, the pavement spreads and brightens, and suddenly it's as if you're going down a grade the way the buildings climb in brick and stone and clapboard. Side streets flicker past you, mouths that open and then close. The traffic moves just fast enough to make it seem as though the people on the sidewalks have been stilled. They move like heat ghosts, masses of them in the early afternoon, shimmering as they slide back out of view. You see in pieces only—the glint of unsunned flesh and well-buffed shoes, sagging trousers, here and there a cuff caught in a sock, arms lagged for children who swing behind, soft slung convexities, dewlapped collars, eyes cast inward on an abstract universe, jackets hiked back on the waist, old men losing rectitude, their faces furred and knotted, heel-tilted women bent into their parcels, girls flounced and shimmed against the tug of earth, ears riding high above the neck on teen-aged boys, hair taut, collisions neatly brushed aside, the very air of cool on some, on some the faintest touch of rage or joy, on most the everyday extinction of fatigue. And all redoubled by the windows that you pass.

Yet this is just the outward look of things. The city is a secret, not a place. Buildings glisten with concealment. Stores tease you with the merest hint of inventory. Couples disappear quite knowingly within an edifice that's possibly a mosque, a tomb, a planetarium, but is actually a bank. Whole gangs of women vanish through an archway as other women exit, laughing. Distracted figures crabwalk up the steps of City Hall, but what they do once there is anybody's guess. Men with tipped-back hats and lit cigars emerge from sunken entrances; they pause to thumb their belts and ascertain the angle of the sun. A corner door beneath a neon sign swings open and all that's visible inside is darkness, a bit of apron, and a glowing cigarette.

Parts of Buffalo turn out to be so orderly they make you want to pray. Grass so neatly shaven, curbs so keenly swept, homes so high above your sense of household that it leaves you breathless. The doorbells on these mansions must go "Pssst" when rung or better yet "Ahem." These avenues are where the city stores its silence, iced among the juniper and holly. Each object here is picked out in its detail, as if someone burnished all the shadows nightly, as if a window had been lifted and the pane no longer blurred the scene's relief. Beneath this canopy of boughs the time must always feel like early morning.

Elsewhere, rows of shingled homes peer open-eyed at rows of shingled homes across the street. Old women knit in second-story sleeping porches; a painter rolls a stucco wall; a young man mends an awning; a grocery van stands double-parked beside a coal truck. The yards, though neat, are scuffed with children's play, and nearly every corner has been cut off by the trail they take to school. Some houses bloom with marigolds, azaleas, or hollyhocks; in one, a bald man facing inward rests his pate against the window—his scalp is an emulsion on the glass. For miles, elm borders alternate with open blocks of sandstone-colored shops.

Every street in Buffalo leads to a street that leads down to the river or the lake; that is its miracle. The city is laid out like the sun half set upon Lake Erie, each major thoroughfare a ray that pulses outward from the disk. At every corner on a grade you look downhill for water, with little luck at first. An ornamental reservoir deceives you. A bridge turns out to span a railway. What you hope is not completely clear, but you've been warned: a viscid surf a couple of inches high will roll in from Toledo.

At last you pull up to the lake and park to look around. This is no ocean, no breaker-beaten shore. On this calm summer's evening, the waves deposit themselves submissively, like bathers lying down on hot sand. The Falls are fifteen miles away and more, invisible, inaudible, if unforgotten.

A freighter under easy steam, making for the harbor, catches your gaze and turns it southward. The shoreline arcs toward the west as gently as the planetary curve. Down there, trenched into the land side of that arc, lie the ship-filled cisterns and aqueducts that serve the factories of Buffalo. How far westward would you have to sail from there before nature reclaimed the waters as its own? And how far south or east would you have to travel before industrial tundra returned to cropland or woods? These are not questions you give much attention to. For even a city of furnaces is beautiful in the light of a falling sun. The brick fires as if it were still in the kiln, the glass as if still in the oven. The buildings of the city proper— Buffalo—glow like ingots of steel, and all its people turn rubicund under the leaves of its worshipful trees.

◆

Buffalo, not Ararat, was the city that got built in the end. If Ararat had risen too, one might have seen it from the Peace Bridge, an Oriental cast to its spires, its rooftops shimmering even in the fog, no doubt. Buffalo and Ararat are twinned cities of the American mind, the one a welter on a freshwater sea, the other an ideal Byzantium on a low wooded island just upstream of a cataract. Buffalo's only destiny was to exist and thereby grow flawed, which is the precondition of all human beauty. But Ararat? The arc of its fortunes is closed in a circle, immaculate, sterile.

Every city is a simulacrum of the world as it is locally imagined. Buffalo's was the world where, for better or for worse, the fear of conquering matter was conquered. Ararat was to have been a city of refuge from a world without refuge. It is no wonder that it never got built, for it was antinomical from the start. Like Jerusalem and Rome, it would have had palpable ties to the next world. What bridge could have linked it to Buffalo? What island could have contained it? What expanse of water could have sheltered it from the mainland?

Barely a month after Mordecai Manuel Noah returned to Manhattan in September 1825, the Erie Canal opened in Buffalo. It was to be the foundation of the city's fortunes, the source of its oratorical fate. Again the village paraded with music and dignitaries. Again there were prayers and speeches. This time the press and caterers got it right. A packet boat called the *Seneca Chief* took on board three barrels of Lake Erie water (one red, one white, one blue) to be ceremoniously mingled with the waters of the Atlantic. By previous arrangement, cannoneers stood poised beside their cannons in a line all across the Empire State. At the instant the Canal was opened by Governor

DeWitt Clinton, a cannon fired in Buffalo. As the rumble
from the shot rolled in like distant thunder across the au-
tumnal treetops, the next cannoneer fired his cannon in
turn, in turn, in turn. It was an unambiguous signal and
a hopeful prognostication. It took eighty-one minutes for
the sound to reach the ears of New York City.

One imagines Mordecai Manuel Noah walking on lower
Broadway in Manhattan that day, dispensing enthusiasm
like small change among the chaos of its people. One imagines him stopped on a busy sidewalk, caught in the toils
of some resonant debate with a whiskered, tobacco-stained
adversary, when the muffled sound of a single cannon shot
made him pause from speech. Would he have remembered
its meaning? Would he have lifted his hand to his ear? And
would he have mourned Ararat, its moonlit domes and its
refugees, before resuming the conversation?

EDDIE

The days are distinct, but the night has only one name.

Elias Canetti

In 1942 Eddie Wenzek went off to the part of the war they were holding in Ithaca, New York. On Christmas Eve his train home, the train to Buffalo's New York Central Terminal, was among the last to depart. "White Christmas," a hit that season, played over and over on the public-address system in the background, resounding more and more hollowly as the recruits from Civilian Pilot Training, like Eddie wearing stout green Civilian Conservation Corps uniforms left over from the Depression, loaded their duffels into railroad passenger cars and steamed off through the southern tier of New York State,

bound for Manhattan. Waiting for the Buffalo train, Eddie
was left standing almost alone on the platform, so lost in
the semitones of Irving Berlin's melody that afterward it
always reminded him of Ithaca. The next morning he
would be celebrating Christmas above the tavern at 722
Sycamore Street with his father and mother and two sisters, who had said repeated novenas for him and for his
brother, Julian, ever since he entered the service. Theirs
was not the easy secularity, the bathrobe Christianity, one
heard in Bing Crosby's voice, but a stricter, efficacious
faith. They prayed Eddie right out of combat.

For a few months it looked as though Eddie might find
himself, as he hoped, in the cockpit of a Navy Air Corps
fighter, flying missions from an aircraft carrier or from an
island airstrip somewhere in the South Pacific. During
CPT at Cornell, he and his new friends learned to fly Piper
Cubs. They attended ground school at Colgate University
and the University of North Carolina at Chapel Hill. Their
platoon leaders were professional athletes, baseball players
mostly, and a wrestler from Buffalo named Ed Don
George, who took responsibility for the platoons' physical
training. ("Who the hell ever wrestled?" Eddie wondered.)
Eddie taught the men of his platoon how to dive under
burning oil, a move he had perfected on the East High
School swim team and in the shallow waters of Lake Erie
off Crystal Beach, where before the war he capered in a
high-waisted, girdle-tight swimsuit, with a pipe in his
mouth and a pair of polished street shoes on his feet.

Chicago was meant to be a hop en route to Pensacola
for Advanced Flight Training, where the nearness of war
might begin to be felt. But in Primary Training, flying a
sturdy biplane called an N3N, Eddie failed a check flight,
a test of fighter-pilot skills. As he attempted a simulated
carrier landing on the Illinois prairie, a strong sense of
reality overwhelmed his imagination. He landed safely, but

when he returned to the hangar he saw that the all-important arrow determining his future as a Navy pilot pointed downward. So Eddie transferred to the Army Air Corps.

After a layoff at home, Eddie was assigned to Miami, then Laredo, where despite the Army's promise he found himself in gunnery school with no further prospect of flight training. He spent weeks shooting clay birds out of the Webb County thermals with a twelve-gauge shotgun, honing his imagination, pretending his targets were Zeros and Messerschmitts dipping and fluttering in the convection mirages. The recruits aimed at each other's pigeons in frustration. They trained without eagerness in the turrets of B-24s, plastic blisters which in combat gave one a hemispheric view of a hostile sky. No one wanted to be a gunner. When pilots needing flight time turned up at the base, gunnery students flew south with them, firing bursts from their twin fifty-caliber machine guns at Mexican ground targets. Eddie was stationed at La Junta, in the dry grasslands of southeastern Colorado, when the bombs detonated over Hiroshima and Nagasaki in August 1945. The Army asked him to join the occupation forces in Europe. "Forget it," said Eddie. "I gotta go tend bar." He was on Sycamore Street by December.

There were not many souvenirs from Eddie's unusual war—a flight certification, menus from nights out on leave, snapshots taken beside a Piper Cub, studio proofs of Eddie in uniform. Wearing double-breasted dress blues, an anchor emblazoned above the glossy bill of his white Navy hat, a single star on his coat sleeve, Eddie appears almost lost in ageless and unaged clothing, all creases and deep shadow. Seeing him thus is like seeing a casual, cursive signature set up for the first time in type, a slim Garamond neatly balanced by serifs on the top and bottom. He smiles without a touch of hardness or nascent militancy.

His is the self-respecting, equanimous gaze of a man who considers the highest earthly rank to be that of civilian, a man for whom all the grades and ratings of the U.S. Navy could be reduced in principle to two: sport and sucker.

In the years immediately before and after the war, Eddie sold Christmas trees outside the bar. He leaned one row of evergreens along the yellow clapboards on the east side of 722 Sycamore and another row along a rope strung between two utility poles. Customers walking up Herman Street brushed their way through a one-lane forest, the air spiced by the scent of resin on bark and by needles crushed underfoot in the snow. Late one Christmas Eve during the kind of snowstorm in which every flake turns variously, indecisively, in the arc of a streetlamp, a beat-up car stopped at the curb. The driver looked over Eddie's remaining stock—a couple of scrub trees, withy and scant —and asked how much apiece.

"Two-fifty," said Eddie.

From the dark window of the car came a tale about the driver's disappointed kids, a tale that included as evidence the dilapidated vehicle, the Christmas spirit, the lateness of night, the falling, turning snow. So, said Eddie later, "I go for the story."

"O.K., one-fifty."

Eddie roped the tree onto the car's roof and the driver handed him a ten. "Now this was a time," explained Eddie, "when no one was carrying tens."

"I thought you didn't have enough money," he said, making change.

"I never told you that. I just didn't want to pay two-fifty for a skinny Christmas tree." And the driver pulled away into the darkness.

The sucker is the one who goes for the story. It reflects a pearlescent beatitudinal quality, pure only in those whose faith is so strong that when skepticism is finally prodded from them it breaks out at precisely the wrong time. The rest are sports and suckers by turn, up one minute, down the next. (Though they perturb it, women generally fall outside the system.) On the night in 1946 when Tom Wenzek threw the bash he had promised five years before—a welcome-home party for neighborhood GIs—Eddie stood behind the bar with his dad, mediating the doings, mixing drinks, emptying ashtrays, wiping up spills, making certain he kept ahead on clean glasses, happy to be at the pivot of such a meaningful confabulation. On that night, the Thomas Wenzek Restaurant overflowed with former servicemen dissevering themselves from rank, if not from the memory of war. That night they shed their hashmarks and pips and dissolved in a two-room, undifferentiated sea of bliss, content for a time to be distinguished only by their root unlikeness to the opposite sex, by their preference for whiskey or beer, by their uncanny resemblance to the sports and suckers returning their stares in the marble-framed mirror behind Eddie's head.

To an immigrant like Thomas Wenzek, Americanization meant effacing the marks of the smaller group and putting on the marks of the larger—learning the common language, adopting the common dress and social conventions in order to blend into the native-born mass. (He never completely succeeded: his diet, his accent, his cursory mustache gave him away.) To Eddie Wenzek, Buffalo-born, the war came as a kind of redundant Americanizing, the sort of experience that convinced him to switch from the whole hog his father served at the bar's semiannual pig roast to a neatly rolled boneless center loin of pork—easily sliced, equitably served—though with the pork he still dished up homemade sauerkraut from the salt-layered barrel in the basement.

Discharged from the Air Corps, Eddie returned with relief to the life of a private citizen, a layman, a future

commoner in the City of God. He became a constituent
of the larger group, whatever it happened to be, a believer
in the intrinsic merit of its majority, an article, after all,
of American faith. (He joined a fraternal society called the
International Order of Red Men, but after a while, he said,
"the Genesee Tribe just pooped out.") By late 1947, when
his father had retired to the euchre table under the Sycamore Street window and Eddie and his brother-in-law
George had hung out the fat neon sign that read "George
& Eddie's," Eddie was a figure of auspicious generality, a
member of men who wear ties to work and a shoe upon
each foot, of persons who shovel the walk while snow still
falls, who drive with a hat on, and who pray on their knees
at bedside. This, it so happens, is an excellent résumé for
a bartender.

Friday night in the Ninth Ward in 1947 might begin Friday
morning, with a haircut. Say you're Eddie—the hypothesis
of a lifetime. On the other hand, say you're not, for on a
late Friday morning in 1947 in the Ninth Ward, where the
taverns have always closed at 3 A.M., Eddie Wenzek is still
sleeping. Say you're Eddie Pajonk, Eddie Wenzek's cousin
down on Clinton Street, south of the railyards. But then
again, say you're not, for Eddie Pajonk is probably either
walking the picket line with the CIO at Worthington Pump
or doing a little farm labor in the outlying countryside in
order to make car payments during the strike. Say, in fact,
that you just happen to be a nameless friend of Eddie
Wenzek's from the neighborhood. Drafted in early 1945,
you are only lately back in town from the duty Eddie
declined at war's end—policing the dismembered German
state, watching a miserable equilibrium descend over Europe. You have yet to figure out exactly what to do with
your GI Bill and the rest of life. Your inclination so far
has been to smoke cigarettes and swap tales over a beer.

But the haircut. You might walk up to Phil's Barber Shop at 779 Sycamore, where Eddie and his dad usually go for a trim. Or you might take the streetcar downtown to the Hotel Statler barbershop for a regular big-city cut. At the Statler any downstate tonsorial wrinkle is likely to turn up sooner than out in the neighborhood shops, where you sometimes feel like a churchyard box hedge due for a midsummer shearing: they square the corners, level the top, rake out the dead leaves, and you're done. Not so at the Statler. There the barber takes your skull in hand like a turnip, appraising it coolly for unexpected lumps and notches. By the time he finishes with the scissors and comb, his fingers hover over your scalp as if it were a crystal ball which with some gentle hand-waving (and a little tonic) might tell him whether to add another chair to the shop or to replace the manicurist with someone who reminds him less of a convent hospital nurse. The barber's own hair, which looks like an aquatint of moonlight on surf, is almost enough to take your mind off the shoeshine being administered by a black man with gold-rimmed glasses and an ocher-toned scar on one cheek. Just when you think he's done buffing, he puts a little procrastinating fluid on his rag so the cut and shine come out even in time. (One of your cuffs has caught in a sock and he plucks it out.) Your shoes glow like coal in the shop mirror, your hair like bronze. It's a shame to put on a hat.

As the streetcar clatters homeward out Sycamore you notice a small crowd loitering near Jerry Pelczynski's place on the corner of Johnson Street, three blocks west of George & Eddie's. Jerry is another old friend, a guy who knows all the ballplayers coming out of the Johnson Street playground, which has been rich in ballplayers. (They end up assembling Fords in the long run.) Jerry has his share of stories to tell. He was one of the first eighteen-year-olds to go to war from Buffalo: Alabama for basic, then

San Francisco. The day comes and he's standing in line
with three or four thousand other soldiers ready to board
a troopship for the South Pacific when he hears his name
being read over a loudspeaker. They tell him he's not shipping out. He had some bridgework done in the service and
they'd accidentally sent the plates to Alaska. "So instead
of shipping the plates to me," he says, "they ship me to
the plates."

Jerry spent the war encoding and decoding in the Aleutians, where there were no women and no trees. Errol
Flynn toured and the men gave him a silver fox pelt. Mar-
tha O'Driscoll—star of *Forty Little Mothers* and *We've Never
Been Licked*—toured and the men stole her underwear.
While Jerry was in the Aleutians he dreamed a Buffalo
dream. His ambition was to build a bar called the Rain-
barrel Inn, a cask-shaped tavern with a sprinkler system
on the roof so water would spill down the sides just as it
does on a real rain barrel standing at the foot of a down-
spout. Big doors, rustic interior, two levels where he
would serve nothing but beer—beer from all over the
world. His eyes practically mist when he talks about it.

Instead Jerry runs a tavern called the Governor's Inn. At
the end of the war, he took a friend in the bar-fixtures
business into a vacant building and said, "John, fix me
up." So John builds a backbar and a frontbar, puts in stools,
chairs, tables, refrigerator, stove, and fryer, then asks for
a check for $7,500. Jerry says, "John, I didn't say I had
any money." Two years later he's just finished paying off
John with interest, a good investment all around. The Governor's Inn stands on land once owned by the boss of
Buffalo's largest shoplifting ring. You'd tell him what
make suit you wanted, what size, whose window it was
in, and he'd tell you where to pick it up. No alterations.
Same went for cops, only they ordered parkas and leather
jackets instead of suits. Jerry had planned to name his bar

the Viennese Inn, but his father, "the Governor" to the family, died just before it opened. So, Jerry says, "what better luck could I get than to use his name?" Now he has pictures of the forty-eight state executives on his walls. The day Jerry opened he was working out of a cigar box with $300 in change on loan from Helgath's Bakery, where all the local bars get their kimmelwecks, pumpernickel, and rye. They offered him a cash register too. It's that kind of neighborhood.

The crowd at the Governor's Inn is heavy with Irish bricklayers and roofers as well as shiftworkers from the Trico windshield-wiper plant. Everyone gets along fine on their way to work in the morning, but by the time they head home in the afternoon they're all squabbling over unions. It's the kind of place where Iron Talem, a wrestler with a head like a roller-coaster, comes in for lunch. He takes a loaf of Helgath's rye, a ham from the butcher across the street, cuts himself ten sandwiches, and downs them with four schupers, twenty-ounce glasses of beer. At Jerry's place they love to play games. You walk in and everyone's drinking with his left hand. You pick up a beer with your right hand and you have to put a nickel in a jar, which goes toward a party in a grove in the summer. The Governor's Inn opens at 8 A.M. (like all the bars on the East Side), and every morning Jerry finds the same woman at his door, shaking. He pours her four ounces of whiskey. She removes her scarf, drapes it behind her neck, takes one end in one hand, clasps the other end against her drink, and pulleys the tumbler up to her mouth. Every night Jerry sends her home with a small Seven-Up bottle full of whiskey. His customers—including those waiting at the door right now, late morning—drink like clockwork, drink to get drunk. It's that kind of neighborhood too.

Standing on Johnson Street there is an aimless knot of foot shifters, luck wavering, frail patience unevenly distributed among them. A few are older men thrown out of work at the end of the war. The others, men and women both, are of the kind that any heavily populated district casts up when the streets have emptied of workers bound for factories and offices and schools. Several might be passing shoppers, except for a fallen hem that seems too consistent with the dented hat and the frayed purse strap. Several could be, and probably are, retirees from a clerk's life, still disoriented, as, in a way, you are too, by the vacancy of these late-morning and early-afternoon hours when all the beds in Buffalo are empty and all the jobs are filled. But every one of them is a person for whom even a single free beer improves the week's economy, and that is what they've gathered for: the arrival of the goodwill man.

Stan Wydro, a vet who fell into the job, is the goodwill man at George & Eddie's. The goodwill man at the Governor's Inn is Lefty Waller, a former ballplayer. Both work for the William Simon Brewery. Their job? To drive from tavern to tavern where Simon Pure Beer is on tap and to spend a little company cash in each place, not a kickback, of course, just a return on interest, so to speak. They buy a couple of rounds for those assembled (and wherever they go they find bars preternaturally full), upping the take in every establishment they visit, checking on the palatability of the company product, giving the company a common touch and a Buffalo accent (that flat "o," as in "bax of chacalates"). You hear guys wondering in amazement at the luck of the men who acquire these jobs. Little do they know.

It's also the problem bartenders face. Everybody wants the job and nobody understands it. Take Al Kirst, the fastest barber on the East Side—a shop at Fox and Genesee. Always came into Tom Wenzek's place, always wanted to be in the bar business. So it ends up he buys a saloon out on Lake Shore Drive, starts drinking too much, and blows up like a balloon. Nobody gets it. To be successful in this business, Eddie Wenzek says, "you gotta stay off the booze and the broads." Which is not how most fellows picture it.

Same for goodwill men as for bartenders. Stan Wydro, for one: almost totally abstemious, a good man. It's no wonder, with him all day, every day in and out of bars, watching people like the crowd outside the Governor's Inn trying to make their presence seem like coincidence (the way puddles in the rain are coincidence), trying to hide their eagerness under a nonchalance that vanishes the moment a free beer begins to froth in the glass. It resembles the scene you see at an ice-cream stand in Tonawanda on a hot July night: under the amber parking-lot lights a heavyset man carries a cone the size of Liberty's torch to his heavyset wife waiting in the car, and as she extends her arm through the open window for the cone her head tips back and her mouth falls open, tongue loose, out of simple desire. If you understood the job of the goodwill man, it would make you abstemious in a hurry. You would have to love people, despite their flaws. You would have to love trading quips, dropping sly hints, winking at yourself with lines like "When *you* have sex it's the Fourth of July. When *I* have sex it's Thanksgiving." You would have to be able to stand the gaff. Otherwise you would wish for a desk job, pronto, where the smell of beer wasn't so strong.

In the afternoon, you see a man about a dog and a woman about a cat. Before long the sun has fallen far aslant and it's time for dinner. You shower and put on a good brown suit and a tie.

"Beautiful" is a word heard in Buffalo whenever fish fry is served, which on the Polish East Side and the Italian

West Side is Fridays from lunch until the commercial kitch-
ens close at midnight (and the hex on meat is lifted), fifty-
two times a year. Eddie uses the word. You do too. When
the backroom waitresses at George & Eddie's walk by with
fish-fry platters held high in the air, you hear the murmurs,
"Beautiful," whenever anyone catches a glimpse. They
don't mean the waitresses, whose waists are cinched by
aprons of chiffon adorned with appliquéd flowers and em-
broidered waistbands. They mean the food. The murmurs
only intensify when a platter lands in front of you: half a
deep-fried Lake Erie blue pike or George & Eddie's specialty, French-Fried Shrimp, made with a batter recipe
taken from Foit's, down on the lakeshore. ("These are real
shrimp, not the butterflies," say Eddie's customers.) With
the fish comes a tossed salad, a cup of cole slaw, homecut
French fries, a plate of pumpernickel bread (Helgath's)
with butter, all for forty-five cents. At that price, you're
allowed to fill your mouth with the crust and the white
flake of fish, a little of the cole slaw possibly, and then say
"Pboofl," still chewing, when asked by the waitress if
everything is O.K.

Everyone gets busy dividing bites. Some diners dive
right in. Some, before tasting a morsel, bestow a consid-
erable amount of time on preparing their plates. First they
use the shaker with a loose-wristed motion—salt falls like
an early Christmas. Then they bulldoze their food into
comestible continents—alps and plains and intimate, cul-
tivated valleys—over which they pause briefly, compas-
sionately, saying an inward, toothsome grace, blessing the
substance of the aerial view beneath them to the nourish-
ment of their already well-nourished bodies.

At the table beside you a businessman has been telling
a story in a hushed voice to a pair of cronies, a story
involving a Jesuit, a rabbi, a Baptist preacher, two strip-
pers, and a kangaroo. After five minutes he has finally

come to the punch line. "So the rabbi turns to the Jesuit and says," and just at that moment, just when the story is tilting on its fulcrum, he shoves a forkful of fish fry into his mouth. It was a trick known to Homer. The cheeks puff up, the tongue does its work aided by the eyes, which bulge slightly in the head to suggest the presence of beauty. Fish fry *is* beautiful. And holy. You could go to a museum and see a "Descent From The Cross" in polychromed lime-wood and next to it a "Fish Fry" carved in white pine with a deep-fried patina, the wood shavings especially brilliant the way they resemble cole slaw.

The blue pike (real name, walleye) comes by truck from Barcelona, a town down the Erie coast, to a local fish shop called the Baltimore Fish and Oyster Company. (The own-er's sister and brother live in the Campanile Apartments on Delaware Avenue—Buffalo's Waldorf, Eddie calls it— but the owner stays over the store on Genesee in case of piscine crises.) People take weekend outings from Buffalo to Barcelona "just to look at the beauty," as Eddie says, by which he means the way the waters unfold to the west beyond the shale bluffs and the mouth of Cattaraugus Creek. That is also why customers jam George & Eddie's, as they had when Freda presided in the kitchen: to look at and devour the beauty with two or three Manhattans or Rob Roys during dinner and coffee and ice cream after if room allows. You eat your fish fry with a Manru Beer ("Make Mine Manru")—luxury suds named after Pade-rewski's only opera—which is made by a local brewery called Schreiber's (real name, Pisarcik: both mean "writer"). You happen to know that the Schreiber's good-will man drives a Lincoln.

The crowd at dinner is a diverse one, just as Eddie has hoped it would be, some folks from the neighborhood and some from nearly anywhere in Erie County. The room rattles with activity, a busboy and three waitresses dashing between tables, disappearing into the kitchen, where you can only imagine the turmoil: a cook, a dishwasher, and two girls who do nothing but set up plates, all sharing that tiny space with a fryer big enough to dunk a six-foot sturgeon in hot oil. The waitresses, hair tightly coiffed into chignons and plaits, swim through the crowd into the barroom to pick up their drink orders at the waitresses' station, which looks like a ladder dangling from the stern of a Niagara skiboat. (In winter the restaurant grows even more crowded—coats are piled on radiators and heaped on coatracks as steam rises from a floor puddled by men clomping the snow off their galoshes and by women stamping their high-heeled rubbers.)

The carriage lamps on the walls have been dimmed. The dark wainscoting and the black spinet and the mirror make the backroom feel more cavernous than it is. At one table sit four teachers who come here weekdays on their thirty-six-minute lunch breaks but who have stopped in for dinner after a late committee meeting. At another table some of the department-store crowd from Broadway have gathered. You might see a couple of familiar faces from the ice factory around the corner or the silk mill on Guilford Street. Buffalo Forge has a couple of men here. Three priests, for whom this is a regular hangout, have walked over together from the Buffalo Diocesan Preparatory Seminary—known locally as the Minor Seminary—near Humboldt Parkway. Whole families wait in the bar. There are a steamfitter named Graf and his wife, Isabel, and a well-known sportscaster. Of some of these people, your mother would say, pityingly, "That person has gland troubles." To which your father would say, "You bet. Mouth gland."

While you eat, an older man with a military haircut appears at the door, waves solemnly at Eddie and Bill Brenner (a genial minor-league pitcher who lives with his

mother and fills in at the bar), and sits down beside Tom
Wenzek in the front room. Before he can get to his own
table the waitress has laid out his food for him. He eats
quietly, rapidly, with medicinal seriousness. After a few
minutes, he pushes his plate away, sidesteps into the
kitchen (he compliments the cook), and meanders out the
door to Herman Street. (Tomorrow morning, sober, he
will sheepishly return and pay his dinner tab.) He is a
retired one-star general of infantry who lives at the Buffalo
Athletic Club during the winter and at Crescent Beach,
Ontario, during the summer. He is another particle of sand
in the postwar drift.

You leave a tip, pay the check, and promise Eddie to
come back later, when a different crowd will have filled
the front room, men who have shaved themselves glossy
but for eyeliner mustaches, women shellacked from bottom to top, their lips so crimson they print up black in
snapshots. You say hello to the people you know, pausing
by their tables as you squeeze past them, trying to keep
your coattails out of the tartar sauce.

As you step onto the walk, the door swings to behind
you and there is a sudden hush. The evening has been laid
in like a berm against the yellow sides of 722 Sycamore
Street. There is a feeling you always get when you leave
a crowded restaurant—a sense that security lies at your
back, behind you in the dining room. The knowledge that
people linger there eating (even when you can no longer
hear them) warms you like a fire. You would get the same
feeling if everyone in George & Eddie's had come there
not to dine but to nap, with plenty of snoring and drooling
and charley horses in the neck, and if you, one of the first
to awake, had walked out onto the street with the night
yet to come. Behind you, you would still feel that chorus
of organisms slowly breathing, dreaming erratic half
dreams, waking to the tingle of frozen limbs, even as you

turned up the next block and wandered away under the elms.

You light up a Chesterfield. The sign "George & Eddie's" glows in the twilight. Once you get over its newness, it too will radiate warmth and a sense of safe haven. There is no getting around the changes at 722 Sycamore Street, the way Eddie has brought it up to 1947. The times have altered and the corner has altered with it. It was all implicit in a scene you remember from childhood. Halfway home from Mass at Transfiguration Church one Sunday morning, you saw the Wenzeks drive past in the family Buick, Tom on the passenger side, Freda next to him, Julian, Jean, and Florie in the back, Eddie in the driver's seat, though he was just a kid, fourteen at most. Tom wore the look of a man who was remembering himself at Eddie's age but who could not make that picture coincide with what he was seeing before him. Eddie was pure futurity. In his eyes there was no past. There was only the road ahead, one hand on the wheel, an elbow out the window, an appreciative audience on both sides of the thoroughfare, walking, like you and your parents, in the general direction of Herman Street, two blocks away. But to Eddie it was no two blocks. It was the infinite westering vector of time, and he was at the wheel.

What the changes at 722 Sycamore really betoken is a shift starting to take place all across the city of Buffalo. Nobody ever drove to Tom Wenzek's restaurant; they came from around the corner, down the street, across an alley. To get to George & Eddie's, they think nothing of motoring from Amherst, Cheektowaga, West Seneca, Lancaster, even the Falls. In his dad's day, the corner bar was truly, as Eddie says, the workingman's country club. And it still is—still the kind of country club that attaches to a bowling alley and not a golf course—only now the emphasis is more on country club than on workingman.

Locals frequent George & Eddie's, just as they frequented
the Thomas Wenzek Restaurant. But some think it's too
posh, as if Sycamore and Herman didn't rank a posh nightspot, a corner place where you could have a drink while
wearing a tie, where you could bring a classy date from
out of the neighborhood for something more than a
schnapps and a pickled pig's foot from a jar on the bar.
Tom Wenzek is indeed the workingman's friend. But the
ones who call him that these days are the ones who feel
uneasy when they walk into his son's place with workboots on.

You might never have noticed the vague unease you
sometimes feel since you've been home if you hadn't stayed
on in Europe after the war. There, if they would only look
up from their barrows and shovels long enough to see it,
they would discover that the neighborhood is over, both
the neighborhood as place and as the narrowly bounded
mental horizon the place implied—that antediluvian, richly
manured hothouse from which only a handful of souls
escaped every generation or two, the rest running to seed
at the first opportunity. The war tore down the neighborhood brick by brick, block by block.

Coming home after two years away, you were surprised
most of all by the resolute stasis of the East Side, as if what
had changed since the war began had been merely personal,
with no implications beyond the immediate family: a tele-
gram and a sudden surplus of hand-me-downs too painful
to wear. Familiarity is no longer intrinsic to the old neighborhood but a thing apart. You admire its almost bodily
presence wherever there is a corner you used to pass every
day of your life. You count familiarity's ribs as it stands
there like a dog that thinks it knows you. How carefully
your parents preserved their old-fashioned manner! While
you were away, they turned the house into a Living Thirties Museum complete with full-scale dioramas of "The

Pork-Roast Supper," "Who's Got the Sports Section," and "Sins of the Bottle." You no more see yourself returning in the end to their stuffed-horsehair parlor than you see yourself wearing spats and a derby onto the dancefloor at 722 Sycamore Street.

You can still walk through the Broadway Market, just a few blocks from George & Eddie's, without finding a difference from before the war in anything but prices. Shopping down the row of butchers' stands there—Wardynski, Piotrowski, Redlinski—you could still rebuild a pig from scratch. In the adjoining aisles you still find smoked eels and poppy butter and prune butter and butter lambs in Easter season, still find a portrait of the Virgin or the Infant of Prague taped to every stall, still hear a chorus of Polish voices rising above the throng of shoppers and merchants and gossips, above the pretty young butchers' daughters in blunt haircuts, their hands stained with pork blood, their knives worn to thin slivers of steel, above the rounded profiles whose cheeks and noses under the influence of cold or alcohol turn an even vermilion without the capillary-bursts you see on Irish faces.

These people seem as familiar to you as your very own aunts and uncles, but they share a kinship with the refugees you saw in Germany, a kinship you never knew existed because your parents also pretended that America is pure futurity. There is still a neighborhood here. The East Side still abounds with shops like Gramcza's Cigar Store, whose owner won't sell you a pipe tool: he tells you to take a nail and flatten the point and save yourself a nickel. But here in Buffalo, as in Europe, the neighborhood as they have constituted it is beginning to be over—over, at least, for the Poles whom the East Side has sustained for half a century, as it did the Irish and Germans and Jews before them. No one sees it coming, though it surrounds them, in small ways as yet.

Further downtown, a new wave of immigrants has begun to occupy Buffalo, blacks who drifted up from the
South during and after the war, part of the sea of strong
backs that Buffalo has always required. And if you drive
in from out of the neighborhood for dinner at George &
Eddie's, it only follows that you plan to drive out of the
neighborhood to digest your dinner. That is not biology;
it is engineering—the consequence of new expressways.
If America learned anything in the war it was engineering.

You walk off into the evening to meet a blind date at
Shea's Buffalo Theater on Main Street, practically at the
foot of Sycamore; she is a service buddy's younger sister
who has recently moved here from eastern Ohio with a
couple of girlfriends. Despite the season—it is late
September—there is still a softness in the air. Just yesterday
the Buffalo Centennial Eucharistic Congress—honoring
the Centenary of the Buffalo Diocese—came to an end, a
hundred thousand of the faithful gathering to watch a massive ecclesiastical procession in Delaware Park, where
everyone was grateful for the pleasant weather. For three
days, the Buffalo *Evening News* has run pictures of important prelates, including Cardinal Spellman, alongside
articles with headlines like "Catholic Dentists Urged to
Organize."

If it were ten degrees warmer now, it would be a June-
bug night, the kind of night, hard as it is to picture the
scene, on which your parents first met while dancing at
Colvin Gables. You can no more imagine your father dancing than you can imagine him swimming through ice floes
to the harbor breakwater in March, which he claims to
have done as a very young man. A lifetime of lifting boxes
of newly butchered pork—eating lunch every day on a
loading dock where he brushes away maggots before sitting down—has torqued his body so far out of kilter that
it looks undanceable. Now his idea of recreation is to sit

in a rowboat on Lake Erie with a lantern hung over the side, fishing—drinking—into the middle of Saturday night until the lake freezes over, while your mother, grown stout and given to vapors, spends the evening at her sister's in the duplex next door.

But when your mother was lithe and your father un-twisted, that was where they met: Colvin Gables Open Air Dancing at Colvin Avenue and Eggert Road, not far from the confluence of Ellicott Creek, Tonawanda Creek, and the Niagara River, one of the great smuggling venues of Prohibition. Colvin Gables had a bandstand and striped canvas awnings that could be raised and lowered over the huge unglazed openings in its walls. Cars crunched onto the gravel parking lot in the twilight, the turquoise sky glowing on the skin of their windshields. Dancers paid their money down and were admitted to the smooth wood-strip footing and that jumpy four-beat music. Then after a time they were swept away by two men stretching a rope across the dance floor. If the night was fair, the dancers inside were conscious of being outside too, for a breeze might rustle dresses during a slow number or they might feel the evaporation where their palms had joined. As they stood outside waiting till the floor was cleared of the next group and they could dance again, they grew conscious of how the dusk had magnified into a whining, sawing galaxy of insects and how pleasant it was to be sheltered from starlight by the canopy of a tree, headlamps flickering from time to time in their direction as automobiles arrived or departed.

The movie at Shea's is *Wild Harvest*, starring Dorothy Lamour, Alan Ladd, Robert Preston, and Lloyd Nolan. According to the *Catholic Union and Echo*, which your mother reads every week, "The love story runs parallel to the interesting and vital business of harvesting wheat. Ladd, Preston, and Nolan are members of a rugged harvesting combine crew that gets into all kinds of trouble, including a spectacular wheat fire, brawls with rival combines, and a set-to with irate farmers." The second feature is *Yankee Fakir*. Not a great pair of movies, but at least your date will ooh and aah at the splendor of Shea's itself. And where do you take a blind date, anyway? To Kleinhans to see "The Hour of Charm," an all-girl orchestra under the direction of Phil Spitalny, featuring Evelyn and Her Magic Violin? To Sammy's Knotty Pine, where "Clara Williams, 250-pound singing star, is held over"? To the Town Casino to see the Three Suns, with the Wally Wanger Lovelies and Gloria French, "The Princess of Song"? To St. John Kanty's Lyceum to hear Skitch Henderson? To Frank's Casa Nova, where the 3 Gay Divorcees are opening for Peggy Lee? To McVan's to see a ventriloquist and the Tremaine Twins, "identical dancing girls," with "Shu Shu" Crawford, emcee? To the Stage Door, to the Rex Grill, to Club Annex, Club Moonglo, Club Genesee, Club Rainbow, Club Romay, to the Havana Casino or Anchor Bar? They will all be jammed. For a blind date from eastern Ohio, *Wild Harvest*, *Yankee Fakir*, and an early cab ride home are a safe bet.

But your date turns out to be a young woman of far more appeal and good humor than your buddy ever mentioned. She is still exhilarated by the city's irreducible gravity, so different from the feel of the small town she grew up in, of which she says, if you close your eyes, you can imagine it being swallowed by cornfields. (You close your eyes and try in good faith, but your imagination acts up: you can't get a bead on a small Ohio town or even a cornfield without seeing Dorothy Lamour among the stalks.) To your date, it's as if Buffalo had been built not on the margin of a glaciated plain, a flat horizon in every direction, but upon a promontory from which it masters the fortunes of the surrounding lowlands, which fall away lower and lower the farther they recede from Buffalo. She has a manner of reducing the irreducible to a level you had never noticed before. When it slips out that you happen to know a couple of professional baseball players, she says, "Imagine making a living with a little white ball," which is not the way you ever thought of it.

Drawn by the lure of the unswallowable city, the two of you find yourselves walking through the quiet streets downtown, following the lights at random, window-shopping for things like business machines and surgical supplies and high-pressure valves and pumps. You tell her a few of the standard stories, like the one about jumping off the Peace Bridge into the thirteen-knot current of the Niagara River where it spills over the Onondaga Escarpment and begins its run to the Falls. You tell it, but it suddenly seems like a very long time ago—she would have been in junior high when it happened—and shortly the two of you fall quiet too, content to lift your eyes to the tops of the illuminated buildings around you and to pretend that you can see no less than everything you think you should be able to see.

As you wander, the statuary of Buffalo watches over you like a psalm. Everywhere there are heads of unimpeachable dignity, looking down from friezes and cornices, staring outward from churchyards and monuments—Fillmore, Lincoln, Cleveland, McKinley, lions and turtles, eagles whose feathers look squamous in bronze, Civil War soldiers and sailors, minor deities, euhemerized heroes, bland abstractions. Twin Statues of Liberty high atop the Liberty Bank Building guide boaters to safety, for when the statues line up east and west, from the vantage of the Niagara River, it is a sign to pilot across to the Canadian side and up into the lake. Gargoyles wink from the Post Office. From high on County Hall caryatids salute in their persons the Mechanical Arts, Agriculture, Commerce, Justice. City Hall is emblazoned with women of fierce fertility, women who call to mind their Medusa-like sisters on the walls of the lobby within—Abyssinian busts of Service, Fidelity, Aviation, Railroads, surrounded by muscular murals spouting mottos like "Frontiers Unfettered By Any Frowning Fortress" and "Talents Diversified Find Vent in Myriad Forms." In this part of town you do not run across the bevy of blue-clad Madonnas you find compassionating the East Side, exalting them of low degree, sending the rich away empty. Here you meet sirens of equity and increase. Between purity, industry, honor, and peace, the virtues of downtown Buffalo might chasten you and your date. If you were paying attention. Instead the two of you have been tacitly laying the groundwork for another such night. Too soon it is time to taxi to Soldiers Place, a circle amid the stately boulevards leading to Delaware Park and Forest Lawn Cemetery, domain of a watchful Ozymandian tribe, and to see your date safely to the door of her rooming house nearby, the cab idling incuriously at the curb.

By the time you get back to George & Eddie's, as promised, it is nearly midnight and still warm. Stars are just beginning to appear from under the overcast in the farthest west. Beneath the sign at Sycamore and Herman, faint music hangs in the air amid the static of unceasing chatter and the rattle and ding of a distant pinball machine. From George & Eddie's back dining room a Bavarian trio (violin, accordion, bass) pumps out reedy, slimmed-down versions of swing onto Herman Street, from time to time mixing them with a straight-up polka and what Tom Wenzek used to call "novelty music" on his menu. Presiding over the band and the dance floor is Bill Grzel, violinist and proprietor of Aladdin Cleaners over on Genesee. You straighten your tie and pluck the cuff out of your sock. How long has it been that way?

The screen door squeaks on its hinges and you enter to the general attention of the crowd at the bar, which looks up as for news of the apostle. They are happy to find only you standing there—the scent of your date's perfume suddenly smudged by cigarette smoke—and they raise their drinks in salutation. Eddie, wearing a clean white shirt and a different tie, waves from behind the bar. Tom Wenzek doles out his stern smile from behind a hand of Sixty-six. There are Sis Huetter and her husband, Al, who teaches and coaches football and basketball now but who used to work in New York for Walter O'Malley, screening the clubhouse guests O'Malley invited to Dodgers games when he was out on the town at Toots Shor's or the Stork Club or Leon & Eddie's near Times Square, which is where Eddie Wenzek got the name for his bar. There's Curly Mayer, a butcher's son, but now the owner of a Savings & Loan, here with his missus, who has hair so red it hurts the eyes. Beside her stand Ted Zawadski, who is famous for wearing a trim plaid tux on New Year's Eve, and Lorraine, his school-nurse date, a woman with soft black hair and a lovely figure, at whose place of employ the boys have an unusually high incidence of scrapes and sprains requiring medical attention. Ted is in baked goods; he also runs a liquor store and a billiard parlor at Wilson and Broadway, in what used to be one of the restaurants of the Waldorf chain.

There's Eddie's sister, Jean, a dark, lanky belle, so beautiful she seems to be Spanish, and her husband, George Ditzel, who sold his dairy ("For Better Health Drink Hillcrest Milk—Hillcrest Dairy, Kilhoffer Street") to go partners in the bar (and to get mixed up in the pinball business). They live in the front apartment upstairs. There are Frank Heller, Bill Brenner's pickoff partner at first base, his date, Mary, and Mary's hometown friend, Renee Celline, who has a way of perching saucily on a bar stool and looking as if she were about to say something sharp. While they wait for time to unfold itself, she and Mary waitress at the Lafayette Hotel, one of the most elegant spots in Buffalo. One day Eddie will take Renee Celline to dinner in the main dining room of the Lafayette. She will be so beautiful that he cannot eat his stuffed tomatoes. It is a sign. That night Eddie will propose.

The steam table has never looked more agreeable. Before taking a seat at the bar, you fix a roast-beef sandwich on a kimmelweck—a hard roll studded with coarse salt and caraway seeds—and you lard on the horseradish. Eddie pours a Manru from the bottle and sets it before you. Where the hunger comes from you have no idea, but the salt on your palate and the coppery sharpness of horse-radish and roast beef, muted by the juices the roll has absorbed, taste wonderful. So does the beer, as fresh and as cold as that glinting, bottomless lake in the High Tatra Mountains of southern Galicia where Ulana, the soprano Polish village maiden whom the Gypsy tenor Manru be-trayed under the spell of the yellow moon (a spell to which Gypsy tenors especially are prone), ended her life with a sudden splash, while the audience at *Manru*'s première at the Court Theatre in Dresden, 1901, dabbed at its mascara and the orchestra sobbed in the pit, moments before Manru himself was hurled after Ulana into the same lake by Urok, the baritone sorcerer-dwarf.

Eddie slips down the bar for a minute to tell you a story. A guy goes to the doctor over on Fillmore, an older doctor. The doctor says to the guy, "Here I am about to retire and I've worked on every part of the body but one." Eddie pauses in wonder, spreading his arms, surveying his body. "And there's a lot of parts," Eddie says. You ask him what part the doctor had never worked on. "That part," says Eddie, "was the heel of the foot." It is a true story, and Eddie steps back to the center of the bar to pour a Simon

Pure, which he will also imbue with his sense of the miraculous. Like the doctor, you would, if you sat in a bar long enough, see everything eventually, and especially the heel of the foot. You would, as Eddie says, become a student of human nature. One night a local monsignor the spitting image of Jimmy Cagney insists on tending bar. Who can say no? Some nights you come in and yet another high cleric, Monsignor Nuwer from St. Mary of Sorrows, will be sitting at the bar with Tom Wenzek, the two of them speaking German and sharing a fetid block of Limburger, no one else near.

Who knows what people get up to in bars? In quiet hours, Eddie's partner, George, gambles on the frontbar with the bar dice; sometimes the winners tip his son, Whitey, for bringing them good luck. Sometimes a table gets up an earnest pinochle game, the pot concealed from prying eyes beneath an ashtray. Men play the automatic nine-pin game up front or shovel their nickels into pinball machines, the equivalent of low-paying slots. They love the one-ball machine called "The Future." You drop the steel ball in the proper hole and the bar owner pays you forty bucks. The bar owner splits the pinball take with the guy who runs the machines, a cut of a couple hundred a week. In the black bars down toward Jefferson, the take is so heavy they don't bother to count nickels. The pinball man stops by twice a day, empties the coin box into two canvas bags, and tells the owner to take his pick.

In the riverside saloons, they trade a drunk a shot and a beer for a freshly caught fish, which goes right to the kitchen, does a quick turnaround, and comes out in batter on some customer's plate, who says "Beautiful" as he lifts away its skeleton. Story has it that in the rough shore bars on Grand Island, taverns built on piers out over the river, there still exist trapdoors through which bodies were dumped in more violent days. They float for a second, the corpses, pockets and sleeves bulging with air, then turn slowly, catch the current, and make the short, violent drift to Niagara, the way the rest of Buffalo's sewage did in those days. Maybe they wash up on the banks of the Whirlpool downstream of the Falls or on the cold shores of Lake Ontario. Maybe they hang up on the rocks before they get to the Falls, too late for that piece of luck to do them good, or maybe they startle a hunter who, despairing of ducks in the early light of morning, has been watching the water slip past, his boat anchored tenuously in the eddies near shore.

And what does local myth have to say about bootlegging? It says that if you dived to the bottom of the Niagara River—either the Buffalo side or the Chippawa Channel along the Canada shore—you would find it paved, like an unearthly version of the heavenly city, with liquor bottles tumbled along the sediments when smugglers, who lashed their freight overboard in case of pursuit, cut the ropes and sped away from the law in their famous black boats, more than a few of which ended up on the bottom too, awaiting a day when everything will be revealed.

In the Ninth Ward of Buffalo in 1947, and in all the other wards as well, a Friday night—any night—ends with a drink in hand. It ends with an inflammation, chilled, in a glass—a potable crescendo. But that is one of the ways the corner of Sycamore and Herman has changed. In Tom Wenzek's day, before the war, people drank with a kind of desperation—and a sheer capacity—that has almost been forgotten. They asked for a drink the way an accident asks for a speeding truck. In Tom Wenzek's day, they drank with blatant disregard for anything but the final effect. "Gimme a Johnstown Flood," they would sing out. "Tom, over here, couple Lusitanias." "You know how to make a Smallpox Blanket?" "I need two Hindenburgs, a Custer's Curls, and a Georgia March, no bitters." A bar-

tender was an arsonist in the hayloft. Most nights the con-
flagration could be seen all over the city, men and women
drifting from their quiet houses up the street to the corner
tavern, where they lay down eagerly in the flames, burning
bright as enamel.

But except for a few now—like the woman who pulleys
the 8 A.M. whiskey to her lips at the Governor's Inn and
who wakes up again and again, surprised, on the steel decks
of ships anchored in the harbor, grain elevators rising over
her like tombstones, and from whose swollen fingers in
cold weather the cops cut her rings—the vocation of public
drunkenness is beginning to disappear in 1947, or at least
to turn solemn and inward. Once, it was easier to know
a neighbor's misery than it is now—back in the days when
two and sometimes three East Side houses, each full of
families divided by a maze of thin walls, shared a single
backyard privy and a common woe. There is no longer
the tolerance there used to be, no longer the sense that it
is the East Side against all comers, that a temperance type
is a meddler, that a drunk muttering in the narrow streets
is expressing a point of view all too familiar to the men
and women passing him by. If you took that drunk, the
one slumped against a truck tire, his shoe caught in the
storm drain, took that drunk home and wiped away the
spittle and the vomit, brushed the hair back and straight-
ened up the clothes, gave the syllables pouring from his
mouth a fair articulation, why that drunk might turn out
to be your brother or your mother or your councilman or
your priest, saying things you heard said over the dinner
table every night, where they were called good common
sense. In the old days, Tom Wenzek's days, drunkenness
was just a form of exaggeration.

Times are indeed changing. Eddie Wenzek pours the
cup that inebriates but does not render stinko. A vision of
neatness, he stands behind the bar at his library: Green

River whiskey, Corby's, a local brand called Rewco. Sea-gram's 5 Crown; Schenley Black Label and Red Label. Calvert's, Calvert's Special, Lord Calvert. Black & White, Teacher's, J & B. Hiram Walker 93 and 99. No vodka, no rum, no tequila—no one drinks them. Tom Collins, Hiram Walker or Gordon's Gin. Three Feathers Reserve Whiskey. Stein's Ale, Simon Pure Beer, Lowenbrau on tap, another half-dozen bottled brands of beer in the back-bar refrigerator. On the stainless-steel workstand, Eddie stirs up poems of contentment, mixes sonnets of self-con-gratulation, shakers odes to quiet oblivion. Though the room is a study in angles, bodies canted in all directions, every face turns his way sooner or later, which is why the mirror.

Eddie has everything under control. The men's room is on his left; the hand sink and towel dispenser hang on the wall outside it. He keeps his highball glasses here, his old-fashioned glasses here, his schupers here, his empties over there. He can mate the male and female ends of a half-barrel tap in the basement precooler without spilling a drop. He takes Canadian money at par. He knows every pose his customers use to order a drink, every grace of condescension, every tiny hauteur that needs to be blunted. He knows how to explain that at George & Eddie's there is no book to drink on. He knows how to fend off the constant offers of "Have one on me" and when to lose the bar dice. He knows how to flatter a lonely woman without entanglement or offense. He knows how whiskey will cur-dle and how it will parch and how, when it neither curdles nor parches, it will warm a room full of tired strangers into friendship. He knows that it will put a city to bed when it most needs the rest and wake it up when it most needs the sleep.

This late, Eddie allows himself a drink or two, in ad-dition to the one or two he has been nursing all night long.

Like his father he drinks without getting drunk, but he drinks not even a quarter of what Tom puts away. This late, he will join the mood rather than prompt it, sample the expansive atmosphere in the bar. When the jukebox takes over from the Bavarian trio and a more urbane music—Dinah Shore, Frankie Laine, Perry Como—slackens the tempo, when the crowd thins but the atmosphere thickens, when the line between sport and sucker gets hard to draw, when even his father, abandoned by the last of his old friends, sets the pinochle deck aside and trudges upstairs to Freda, then Eddie has time to be at home in his work, to allow a conversation to ripen, to light his pipe with the lion-shaped head and send its pleasant smoke curling into the air.

What Eddie knows of the world lies at his fingertips. His interests are seated before him. He already walks in the path of his wishes. That the universe is expanding means only that Eddie plans to buy the house next door, knock it down, and put in a parking lot for his customers. It means only that in a bar this late at night the talk may rise from the parochial to the provincial, though in the parochial, as the Church would say, can be found salvation. Eddie bought the business from his father, but at times like this it feels more like an inheritance, like an old family farm. Eddie has abandoned the archaic three-crop rotation, planted new hybrid seed, mowed the ditches, repainted the barn, but the landscape itself has not changed. It encompasses him, waking or sleeping, this canary-colored building. It rises around him like the flowering of a taproot, among whose involute petals and leaves Eddie and a host of spiritual kin have found nurture. To imagine another manner of life would take too much philosophy.

It is 3 A.M. Closing time all over Buffalo. Outside, the night has turned much cooler, with a swirling wind that plucks at the trees and rattles the rose stalks in the side garden. The stars have risen over the whole of the sky. Eddie locks the front door and turns out the lights. He flicks off the sign that says "George & Eddie's," and the corner dims by half. Then Eddie walks back behind the bar and pours another round of drinks, one for himself, the rest for a few nameless friends. They sit in the dark and admire the stillness and the way reflections gradually surface from the depths of the mirror. They listen to the radiators starting to hiss. Before long the bars near the Clinton Street Market, where Eddie buys produce, will open. Farmers who rise in the night, which Eddie has deepened by dousing his sign, will enter those bars just as the heavens go pale. They will kindle that inner fire. They will try to stay warm through the long day ahead.

AN INNOCENT
POPULATION

The ideas of people in general are not raised higher than the roofs of the houses. All their interests extend over the earth's surface in a layer of that thickness.

Nathaniel Hawthorne

Nineteen forty-seven is a man in a brown hat and a good brown suit with the back of one pantleg caught in his sock. That this has been a cold wet spring is on his mind. So is the appearance in March of the largest sunspot ever recorded, not to mention the sudden birth of a nova in Sagittarius or the odd circumstance that this should be a year "unusually rich in comets." He puzzles over a statement that has been troubling his brain: "At no time in history has the steel industry lain down less on the job than during 1947." Has the steel industry had a lying-down history? He marvels that there are "very few large bridges

. . . actually under construction" this year. What does it mean? Have we spanned all the eligible gaps? Hurdled all the rivers and gorges? Or are we waiting till the steel industry lies down less than it has not lain down this year? The brown-suited man stares at his glass. There is a 73 percent chance that the whiskey in it, which should by rights be as mature, if not as complex, as an elementary-school student, is less than two years old. In 1947 there are many reasons to be bibulous. Infant whiskey is not one of them.

Nineteen forty-seven is a man with the back of one pantleg caught in his sock. He wears a good brown suit and a brown hat even in a bar. If he would just straighten his leg, the cuff might fall out of his sock and settle over the vamp of his shoe, where it belongs. But that is the leg whose foot is resting on the raised tile footrest. No one else in the bar will call attention to the pantleg caught in his sock because they all have dill seeds stuck in their teeth. From the vantage of the present the past seems—falsely— a little naïve. To those in the dream, the dreamer always looks like a simple fellow with indigestion, wearing a pointed nightcap. But the dreamer eventually wakes, and his night visions, sprung from Limburger and rye, vanish with the morning air and the smell of calf brains cooking in the kitchen.

The man in the good brown suit with the problem pant-leg has other things bothering him. He has been worrying over the teaser to a story he came upon some time ago in the *Saturday Evening Post*. "It was downright abnormal of Joe," it read, "not to want a new electric refrigerator. It was even more abnormal of him not to want the beautiful girl who was selling them." Well! One's heart went out to Joe, of course, as it also did to John Jones, another magazine character. John was considering cashing in the family's Victory Bonds because his wife, Ellen, was ill.

Luckily, Ellen had not lost her head. She knew what an asset Victory Bonds were; she knew that "even Hirohito would like to be holding American War Bonds" now. So John economized and let them be. "Even after she got better," he said, "I stayed away from the weekly poker game—quit dropping a little cash at the hot spots now and then—gave up some of the things a man feels he has a right to." That is the year 1947 all over: if you're not not falling for a new electric refrigerator and a beautiful girl with a job, you're giving up some of the things a man feels he has a right to. Proud of it, in fact.

In America, the war's cicatrice is a cool ivory now. After widespread strikes in 1946, the country is beating its swords into appliances, its half-tracks into Studebakers— "First by far with a postwar car!" The United States peers into a crystal ball and what it sees is Kelvinators. It sees relief from patriotic abstinence, a whole continent beginning to untruss. It sees the resumption of privacy, if only there were someplace to house it. In its crystal ball, America discovers Naugahyde: "Nothing's too drastic for this plastic!" In every driveway it envisions a De Soto clicking as it cools and in every Whirlpool a day's diapers tumbling dry. Half of what it sees it has never seen before, so it takes counsel about the future wherever it can. With the air of eminent analysts, popular magazines ask, "What first gave you the notion of doing over your living room—or replacing that outmoded refrigerator—months before you did anything about it? . . . Perhaps it was *advertising*." Perhaps it was. Postwar ads paint a future succulent enough to redeem with interest the drab, self-sacrificing years just past. As paradigms for national life in a new age, advertising's benign, iconic predictions are perfect. Any light-house will do in a fog.

Everyone rejoiced at the coming of peace after the chaos of World War II. But who recalled that peace is more formless than war? In 1947, Americans still know all there is to know about destiny and accident, though they are disremembering fast. Napoleon himself could teach them nothing about the motivations of history. The terms of Japanese and German surrender dictate that honor and fate, spoiled by Axis abuses, shall be set aside for a time. Except for freedom and security, most of the great coercions capable of mobilizing a people have been temporarily retired in the West. Saving money for a layette, a Plymouth, and a house in the burgeoning suburbs is all the direction any American needs. The routine peacetime incentives have gone half-forgotten till now, but they begin to be felt again: incentives like plain ambition or a dread of too much stability—something no one has felt for ages—or fear of not making enough of oneself, fear of a lifetime cleaning carburetors down at the gas station where George & Eddie's dinner crowd park, a lifetime spent in one small job, one small set of rooms, contemplating how pathless, if left unexplored, is the wide, sunlit basin of one's days on earth.

"There was never a better time than this to be an American and to be young," said Walter Lippmann at war's end. This time it was apparently true. Life was going to get good. The Forties and its colossal war were floated on the faith of young men and women. We won, the argument ran, so let the getting good begin. Americans, said the director of War Mobilization and Reconversion, "are in the pleasant predicament of having to learn to live 50 percent better than they have ever lived before." Between July 1945 and July 1946, the civilian population of the United States increased by eleven million, mostly demobilized servicemen and servicewomen. They came home eager to enjoy America's physical blooming and to start some physical blooming of their own in the curtained half-light of evening. The sudden adulthood conferred by war bewildered them, as adulthood of any variety would have. So did parenthood, into which they hastened with alacrity. As early as 1943, the birthrate began to rise well above normal peacetime levels. But as a feat of mass parturition, nothing matches 1947, when there are 25.9 births for every thousand Americans, the highest percentage since records were first kept in 1915. Three and three-quarter million consolidations of peace, forever innocent of the world before the Second World War, are born that year to three and three-quarter million recently gravid women whose husbands wear the catastrophic grin of salmon beached on spawning beds. Nearly 10 percent of the total population is under five years old.

It is not just the return to peace and the retooling of American industry for home and highway that gives 1947 its distinctive feel. The war to save the world naturally became a war to change the world. The country's heightened awareness of the globe lapses into a sullen glower in an easterly direction toward the Soviet Union, across the "rubble heap," the "charnel house" of Europe. The once-familiar names of hundreds of atolls and beaches and villages fade from consciousness like high-magnitude stars in the luminous reach of Buffalo's night sky. The coal strikes, rail strikes, telephone strikes, teachers' strikes and auto workers' strikes begin to abate, leaving everyone with a sense of how precarious domestic wartime unity really was and how little selflessness there is to spare on any but the direst occasions. U.S. firms begin to deal directly with German manufacturers again. Eight hundred and forty-five thousand square miles of Antarctica are mapped. Thor Heyerdahl sails *Kon-Tiki* to the Marquesas from Peru. The bones of Australopithecus, a "gracile hominid," are exhumed from South African rubble by a team of gracile hominids wearing short pants and eyeglasses.

Two world wars framed the last period of peace. In the twenty-year span between Versailles and the Nazi invasion of Poland, peace had no future and no useful past. But at the middle of the end of the Forties a future of some yet uncertain kind—prospectively more ingenuous than were Prohibition and the Depression—lies open to the far horizon like an endless tree-shaded succession of unfenced backyards. In retrospect it is easy to see that nearly all the essential elements of postwar America meet together for the first time in 1947. But from within the year it is hard to tell which facts will assume governance and how they will react upon each other in the decades to come. If only one could decipher the newness of the new.

By 1947 the worst of the postwar shortages are over. The Wage Stabilization Board goes out of business, and the cash locked up in war bonds begins to dilate the economy. The departments of Army, Navy, and War merge to form the Department of Defense, with James Forrestal as its first secretary. The Air Force acquires its independence from the Army. America's wartime intelligence services metamorphose into the CIA, and the National Security Council is formed. In May, President Truman asks Congress for funds to conduct an investigation of the loyalty of federal employees, a request that Governor Thomas Dewey declares is Truman's confession that the Democrats need "a $25,000,000 spraying with D.D.T." In October, Ronald Reagan testifies before the House Un-American Activities Committee on the presence of Communists in Hollywood. The Navy fires a German V-2 from the aircraft carrier *Midway*, the first missile launched from sea. At Harvard in June, Secretary of State George Marshall announces proposals for the European Recovery Program—the Marshall Plan.

In 1947 three and a half million automobiles are manufactured in a country where seven and a half million homes have no running water. Railroad traffic declines from a 1944 peak of 95.5 billion passenger miles per year to 45 billion in 1947. A total eclipse of the sun occurs in May, and film of it is broadcast over the "New York-Schenectady-Philadelphia-Washington television network." One hundred and seventy thousand television "receivers" are manufactured, most with ten-inch tubes, though by year's end only seventeen thousand sets (and eighteen stations) are in operation. In October, one might watch the first televised broadcast from the White House, President Truman's spectacles flickering in the lights. "Television Packs 'em In," report magazines that recognize a good thing when they see one. The *Evening News*, reporting the first display of RCA table model televisions in Buffalo, observes that "the room need not be darkened" and that "sound reception is included." "Few other than those highly trained in modern electronics know much about [TV]," says *Liquor Store & Dispenser*. "Only its value can be readily understood."

In 1947 most of the faces in American advertising look like apples newly picked from the orchard in Eden. But there is often one person among them, a man usually, who gives off a different aura, a serpentine sharpness, a look of homemade, jerry-built *je ne sais quoi*, which in '47 is becoming increasingly useful to advertisers as a counterpoint to the beatific joy normally inspired by capitalism. This man would rather be savvy than wise. To him satisfaction is something for nothing. You walk into one of the smart bars in Buffalo—George & Eddie's, for instance—and there he is, straight from a tobacco ad, looking back at you over a woman's shoulder in a knowing way that suggests that all men are platoon buddies in the war of the sexes. He keeps a toothpick in his hatband. He handles cigarette smoke the way Will Rogers handled a lariat. When he sees unaccompanied women, even the lady bowlers sponsored by George and Eddie's—team-drinking matrons who on league Fridays have hearts of Mineralite and a Circean power to humble males—he tries to "give them the business," as Eddie says, or "operate" on them, as if he were a surgeon with a bad conscience and an amphetamine habit. His brown hat dips at a rakish angle. He wears a good brown suit. But when he turns back to the whiskey in the glass on the bar in front of him, you realize he has a pantleg caught in his sock. You watch him carefully. When no one is looking, he lets his savvy drop. Underneath it, he is flummoxed, and you can see that he is just an ordinary 1947 guy with a case of the worries. Why, he can't stop wondering, did Joe not want a new electric refrigerator or the beautiful girl who was selling them?

In the late 1940s, everything was heavier. Turn down the street from George and Eddie's on a snowy afternoon and walk east to the nearest major intersection, the corner of Sycamore and Fillmore. Loaf-shaped buses lay charcoal exhaust trails on the new-fallen snow. A clock bulges outward from the brick façade of Antoinette's Ice Cream Lounge, the minutes and hours ticked by thick black hands. A two-bulb traffic signal sags from an overhead cable. Except for the buildings, the lines of everything manmade are faintly bulbous. Design devolves from the speediest object a culture can produce. In 1947, that object is still, in the popular mind, the B-29, the airship that flew the Hiroshima and Nagasaki missions, a mirror-finished, cigar-snouted, torpedo-shaped bomber with rounded wingtops and sharp lines only on its trailing edges. Sharp lines on the leading edges belong to the supersonic era, which, with the flight of the Buffalo-built Bell X-1, slung aloft beneath the wing of a B-29, begins on October 14, 1947, though the public isn't put in the know until nearly eight months later.

When drivers ease into parking spaces on Fillmore Avenue and kill the ignition, their weighty black autos settle into profoundly inertial states, squatting on wheezing shocks and springs. These cars have the aerodynamics of leather brogues, the contours of a southern politician's haircut. Though their lines sweep back from the vanishing point and their tires hide beneath cowlings, these cars never threaten to take to the air. They tamp the road and furrow the atmosphere. They are stamped from heavier steel than their modern successors. Only the paint is thinner: if you are an ardent polisher, you can wax a postwar sedan right down to the primer.

At Fillmore and Sycamore, everyone seems bound to earth by a stouter rope of gravity. Heels on women's shoes are chunkier, to support the bulkier frames of their wearers, who again and again must choose between a patch of slick ice or an over-ankles walk through a bank of snow, where the footing is better on buried grass. The falling snow feathers gently downward but alights on brown and gray masses of coating, thick-hatted columns muffled sturdily against the chill. They trail firkin-shaped children behind them, forming short lines at the car stops, thrashing snow from their shoulders before entering the doctors' offices that line Fillmore Avenue. The Number 23 streetcar skids past with a dimmed clangor, its windows frosted at the edges. The farther you look down Fillmore the weightier the air seems to grow with the cold, the more gelid the whitened asphalt. The sky overhead is an old boarding-house sheet flapping eastward from Lake Erie.

If you leave Fillmore Avenue and drive out of Buffalo toward the southern tier of New York State, you soon come upon the rolling landscape that advertisers treasure when they need to evoke autumn, winter, Thanksgiving, or Christmas. It is a landscape whose beauty wherever it appears—on calendars, billboards, illuminated beer signs—almost reconciles one to the fact that even in 1947 American advertising is never more unabashedly vulgar than when it portrays the rural past. A bend in the road is a good place to park, to get out of the car and watch the hills unveil the familiar view. The ridges are darkened by mixed woods; the deciduous trees are gray and bodiless against the snow, the pines as opaque as stones. Near the rim of woods stands a small white house with a deepset porch. Behind it, a white barn practically dissolves in the scant illumination. Drifts curl upward toward the firs that edge the house, lights burn in the kitchen, and twilight shadows fall blue on the snow. There is a crimson flush across the hills to the west behind you. Along the valley floor, a dairy farm pastures on a cutbank creek, its faded buildings the color of driftwood. You lean over your car's warm hood, stare across a ditch full of milkweed pods poking through the wind-glazed snow, and consider the future while the past reverberates in the cold dusk air.

One day someone from 1991 will find a 1947 advertisement illustrating this very country scene, the type of ad they will still be making in 1991—one that uses a grandma who bakes and a grandpa who whittles and the reunion of their descendants in a white country house as so soothing a bait that you never feel the sales trap closing till it snaps your neckbone. The person who finds that old advertisement will notice that, even after patent nostalgia has been deducted, the countryside in the 1947 illustration is quieter and more self-contained than the same scene in a 1991 rendering. The reason is obvious. In January 1947, 142 million people live in the United States of America. By 1991, there will be 250 million. It is as if in the coming years the nation were to build fourteen new cities with a population of eight million individuals each. But fourteen new cities will never stay put in just fourteen spots. They will disperse themselves like the runners from a strawberry plant, like the tongues of a prairie fire, until even the plainest landscape is altered, if only by the viewer's regret.

In 1947, a feeling of detachment, of serene isolation, still pervades this clearing. Only a single telephone line threads its way above the fence. The road past the house has been traveled by only a single vehicle driving west, leaving its tracks in the snow. It passed while the sun still lay above the hills—three men, their faces lit up, smiling with dry yellow teeth in the warm, witty room of a pickup cab. It seemed strange to see them coming out of the woods and up the road in your direction, for this is the kind of landscape that one is always meant to be entering, a scene poised like a receptacle. There is no inn in the middle distance to induce coming and going. Around the next set of curves there is no cluster of detached suburban houses moored to birdbaths, no string of bungalows flanked by driveways as black and as smooth as obsidian. There is no highway, just a gravel road that winds through this valley toward a little town that no one has figured out a reason to visit except the usual petty errands. This place you contemplate across the hood of your ponderous black car is not some alternative to a crowded city. It is not an alternative to anything, not one in a set of choices. In 1947 the people who live here do not yet consider living here optional.

◆

After the war, Eddie Wenzek flew a plane of his own, a Cessna 140 he kept at the Hamburg airport. No one was sure in those days where general aviation was headed. Perhaps it would see the kind of spectacular growth that motoring had witnessed earlier in the century. Perhaps families would buy airplanes the way they would soon begin to buy station wagons. But not yet. Flying took money in 1947. Eddie's Cessna was a sign of the percentage that bar owners took from the pinball machines in the bar, the cash that came from the payphone and the jukebox and the highlife in general.

Still, Eddie was no advocate. "Flying's boring," he said. "You fly around, you land, you have a cup of coffee." When Eddie took the Cessna up, he buzzed the bar at 722 Sycamore Street to see how antlike the people on the East Side looked. Everyone at the bar knew who was causing the ruckus overhead: some wandered out to the sidewalk, drinks in hand, to study the underside of Eddie's fuselage on his next pass. If Tom Wenzek happened to be spading shrimp shells into the garden, he'd look up. But after a while the effect was lost, and Eddie, tired of airport coffee and orbiting over Sycamore Street, sold his plane. By 1947 much of the innocence had gone out of the air.

But sometime before the war, probably during the early 1920s, a dirigible had flown over Buffalo. From the ground it looked like a dark bomb-shaped cloud moving west against the prevailing winds under its own power. The low-pitched, ratcheting buzz of its engines was audible only if you happened to cock your head just so. Where the dirigible departed from, whither its course, where it landed—all are unrecorded. But while it was aloft a photographer in its gondola took an exposure of the city— itself like the shadow of a thunderstorm—passing gravely below. The photograph shows part of the captain's hat, a corner of his console, and several of the guy wires that shackled the airship's monstrous girth, which is tangible, though unseen, overhead. The gondola window framed a view that reached down and across the city.

Winter smoke mantled Buffalo. The haze was general, rising from coal stoves everywhere, from ill-filtered sources of warmth whose thick fumes gave the impression that the city was fueled by cattails and green willow shoots. There was enough sun in the sky to pick the gleam off

Lake Erie and the Niagara River and off the ice on house-tops lying perpendicular to the camera's lens. The streets were largely obscured, marked only by ranks of houses and by lines of trees that suddenly spread like inkblots in the parks and cemeteries. At ground level, Buffalo had been blurred by the odd winter light into a single diffuse terrain, as if the city had shifted suddenly while having its picture taken, like an impatient cartboy before his load of branches in a much earlier era. The setting was less city than citydom. This could have been Warsaw, Budapest, or St. Louis, and that gleaming water the Vistula or the Danube or the Mississippi. In the distance, clearly focused, tall brick chimneys steamed beside the lake. And all across that urban expanse, precisely etched above the trees in every quadrant of the view, rose spires and church towers into the lighter mist where the dirigible rode.

Looking down upon Buffalo from that gondola, one would have felt the strong feeling that this indistinct, wintry metropolis harbored an innocent population, a people whose utmost guile was from that height simply invisible. Down among those narrow houses, in that shadowy dry-point of silvers and grays from which steeples emerged like mooring masts for an armada of blimps, lived a people largely unheeding of the skies, for trouble, historically, came around the corner, not over the roof. Day after day, they might be as slippery as could be in negotiations among themselves. Year by year, they might embody every form of every torturous vice and virtue that humans can embody. But from the angle of a dirigible's awkward, lumbering flight, they looked, to a compassionate viewer at least, blessedly innocent, not least because they were being studied unawares, going about their business in the belief that only their own lazy consciences were watching—a city over whom a dirigible might easily creep unnoticed.

To be overflown creates a feeling of vulnerability; one

imagines oneself the object of far-seeing, dispassionate scrutiny. To be the one flying over, the one looking down the flues and across the roofs and into the yards and alleys all at once, to be the one in the dirigible whose unexpected appearance sooner or later makes crowds drift like sheep across a common—in some that stimulates a feeling of dominance. But to others the city's diminished profile against the immense flight horizon serves as a reminder that though the scale of human works increases with time, the stature of men and women does not. Their massed, collective efforts peter out, as they have for centuries, in the pinnacles of the churchtops and at that ill-defined border in the distance where urban streets give way to fields.

Studied closely, that photograph taken from the dirigible resembles a piece of evidence presented before a congressional committee by some good-looking young astronomer in a late-Forties science-fiction movie—an aerial photograph shot by sheer coincidence at the very last moment when life on earth was still normal. Imagine that movie. It was an ordinary day in an ordinary town in an innocent time. The entire city was doing what cities do when the sun is shining and their country is at peace. So perfect was Buffalo's ordinariness, so unadulterated its innocence, that suddenly there appeared in its sky an alien spacecraft, a "flying disc," "flat and round," exactly like the spacecraft spotted over Idaho on the Fourth of July 1947, by a United Air Lines pilot.

This was not some ship of blameless navigators from a benign star (though in the second reel a good-looking young philosopher would struggle valiantly to test that hypothesis). This was a crew of shapeless, foul-smelling space monsters whose evil was the inverse measure of the innocence that characterized this great American city. Even if they didn't destroy or enslave humanity, these spacemen would certainly alter its course. (Their sudden appearance was going to slow house sales in a couple of suburban developments one could think of.) A city only slowly relinquishes the anxiety it felt when it was just a wilderness town, separated by days from civilization as Buffalo once was; now, with strange electrical disturbances cutting off telecommunications and no telling what extragalactic microbes requiring a quarantine, this city would soon be a wilderness all over again. Paranoia was rampant, a condition that innocence cannot survive, just as it can barely endure the thought of far-seeing, dispassionate scrutiny.

To find an innocent-looking population, one need not search from the air alone. Take another example. Early one Sunday afternoon the driver of a red Dodge pickup, traveling at moderate speed out Sycamore Street, swerved to miss a car pulling away from the curb and lost control of his truck. It rocketed across the street and hit the far curb, rolling to the left and skidding on the driver's side into the angled entrance steps of George & Eddie's, like a Dodge-shaped meteorite coming in on a tangent so as to kiss the earth and leave no crater behind. The noise was tremendous. Almost immediately, a crowd began to gather, scarcely able to believe its luck. The pickup just missed the telephone pole and fire hydrant on the corner and the front wall of George & Eddie's itself, yet it came so close to the door that jokes were shortly made about the problem with drive-in saloons. The driver was badly shaken, but no one else was hurt. Eddie, who was upstairs when the accident occurred and who thought it was an earthquake, brought his camera.

The curious came running from the houses that lined Sycamore, as well as from the smaller houses down the peaceful, tunnel-like sidestreets that edged off to the north and south. Then came the police cars and firewagons. Given a routine escapade and a tow truck parked right across the corner at the Mobil station, policemen and firemen were willing to while away an early Sunday afternoon listening to the local wits with as much secret pleasure as the third-base umpire in a home-team blowout at the Rockpile. But the majority of the crowd was children, who had been told emphatically by their mothers and fathers to Go Find Something To Do Till Supper and Stay In The Neighborhood, at which point, as if one could summon the operations of fate, the Dodge keeled over just around the corner.

It was an autumn afternoon, the kind that persuades early risers that winter is coming but which by two o'clock reminds everyone of a fine June day when the soil in gardens has at last taken on useful warmth. Some people had prudently wrapped themselves in wool plaid jackets, others wore shirt sleeves; only the firemen in their knee-length slickers and waterproof boots were uncomfortable. The driver was laid out on the sidewalk and someone's coat had been slipped under his head. The crowd formed a loose semicircle around the pickup, which was naturally of greater interest to them, resting as it did in an extraordinary position, than was its driver. (They had all seen men as dirty as he lying woozy on sidewalks before.) The crowd waited, but nothing happened.

And so, urged gleefully by Eddie Wenzek, who had a proprietary interest in this accident, members of the crowd took turns being photographed beside the pickup's exposed undercarriage, which faced the intersection of Sycamore and Herman. A boy in a cap with earflaps stood proudly in front of the transmission; a young father posed with his daughter beside the differential, the great canary bulk of 722 Sycamore Street looming behind the rust-eaten, dust-caked underbelly of the Dodge. One high-school girl blushed feverishly, drawing her shoulders together, barely able to remain at the focus of everyone's attention—so interesting a sight was daylight on the parts of a motor vehicle where daylight never shines. These snapshots, neatly familiarizing the unfamiliar, resemble illustrations in guidebooks to marine mammals, for some of the rarer whales have been photographed only after washing up on beaches, where they form an irresistible subject for vacationers, who use them as props. ("Look, honey! A dead whale! Let me get a shot of you on its back.")

But not everyone saw the joke. It had been too near a thing. And soon the mood of the crowd turned inward. When the tow truck dragged the pickup back into the street and over onto its wheels, it exposed serious damage to the left front fender and the driver's-side door. The windshield had shattered at impact, and everything in the cab had been catapulted forward. Some people had seen worse, of course. Among those who hadn't, especially the older children, the awareness dawned that this astonishing mutilation of an object of such intimate solidity—just like their fathers' Chevys and Fords—had been caused by ordinary earthly forces of a kind that ordinary people put into effect every time they drove home from Mass on a quiet Sunday morning after stopping for fresh rolls at Zwack's Deli across from St. Mary of Sorrows Church. It was impossible to look at the pickup's splintered left headlight and not to think of one's own eyes. It was impossible to imagine the violence of the crash and not to calculate how much more impressionable than unhealing steel human flesh might turn out to be. As looks registering thoughts like these passed among the crowd, drifting from person to person, one could almost hear in the distance the low-pitched, ratcheting buzz of a dirigible flying between the bell towers and steeples of East Buffalo, navigating high above the accident and the foreshortened multitude standing in the street outside George & Eddie's, high enough so that beyond the city, beyond its smokestacks, clouds appeared to be walking on stilts of light across the shimmering western lake.

◆

"Strange Forces Hold the Universe Together . . . And Oil-Plate Your Engine," said a 1947 advertisement for Conoco's Nth Motor Oil. At first this reads like a standard commercial non sequitur, slightly dizzying in its inconsequentiality. It resembles an ad published about the same time by a Buffalo-area oil company called Frontier, makers of "ATOM-ized" Gasoline: "The Atomic Age Has Arrived . . . So Has This Great Gasoline." Frontier's ad makes it sound as though ATOM-ized Gasoline, like the atomized bomb, was Oppenheimer's baby down in New Mexico, where years of research and millions of dollars had at long last enabled Frontier to put atoms in its fuel. "The Atomic Age Has Arrived . . . So Has This Great Gasoline." The ellipsis, those three meaningful dots, is like a synapse; you can feel a queerly charged sales logic pulsing across it.

Unlike the Frontier ad, the Conoco ad is not as vacuous as it seems: "Strange Forces Hold the Universe Together . . . And Oil-Plate Your Engine." The Conoco slogan is an accidental case of parallax, of shifting perspectives. To a physicist, whose professional gift is never to despair over conflicting evidence, the statement in the Conoco ad is quite literally and mundanely true. At the atomic level, the translucent oil you pour down the filler hole in your De Soto's engine block is indeed an elixir of the universal forces binding matter together all across creation. But to an ordinary motorist, the statement "Strange Forces Hold the Universe Together . . . And Oil-Plate Your Engine" is like a pair of binoculars, either focused at long range or focused at short range, but not both at once. With an effort, you can picture the strange forces of the universe swirling about in deep space, for the ad depicts a suitably lurid galaxy resembling a whirlpool of shining ellipses. But when you are lying on a creeper under the De Soto, loosening the crankcase drain bolt, neck and arms fighting an unequal battle with gravity, hot black viscosity running down your wrist, it is hard to keep in mind that by popping open a quart of Nth Motor Oil with a churchkey, you are also peeling back a corner of the universe.

And likewise, thanks to the etheric power of everyday life over memory and imagination, after you've changed the oil and lowered the hood, you can drive the De Soto down to the local Frontier station—the one where gas is delivered "*fresh daily*" from a refinery that "serves only this Buffalo area . . . making Buffalo drivers the envy of the nation"—and fill it up with "ATOM-ized" Gasoline, all without having to reflect as you stand there talking to the attendant, gas nozzling into the tank, fumes iridescing upward, a Saturday idling all over town, that if "ATOM-ized" Gasoline had arrived the way the Atomic Age did, it would have fallen as burning rain from the sky.

When the United States entered the Second World War, it abandoned moral and political isolationism for good. But there is no abandoning geography. Despite the shock of Pearl Harbor and the invasion hysteria of the war's first months, the nation never surrendered its innate, succoring belief in the security of physical isolation—in the safety of being, with Canada and Mexico, a continent unto itself. No matter how painful the fighting in Europe and Asia became, the actual destruction of combat never carried to America, a fact that was as important, psychologically, to soldiers in the field as it was to civilians at home.

The war opened the world to the United States, but it also opened the United States to itself. Millions of Americans relocated for the duration. They discovered, most for the first time, how vast their country was, and how protective overall that vastness seemed. Job-seekers up-rooted their families and moved to cities where war industries clustered—cities like Buffalo, where they worked at Bethlehem Steel making the substance for tanks, shells, and gun barrels, at Curtiss Wright making the P-40 and the Curtiss Tomahawk, at Bell Aircraft making the Bell Airacobra, at Spreichtool making bomb racks, at the American Car Foundry making howitzer shells, and at dozens of other companies engaged in defense work. Soldiers came from anywhere, trained anywhere, and were deployed anywhere in a seemingly endless shuffling of this country's young men.

Hundreds of billions of passenger-miles were spent gazing out train windows, watching the countryside lay itself out in an endless divergence of scenery broken only by a handful of urban stations. Passing small towns in the night, one could smell kitchen gardens lying behind houses close to the tracks and see streetlamps hanging cones of vaporous light over intersections empty but for a homebound dog with its tongue out. In towns like these—so deep was their quietude—none of the sleeping awoke at the sound of a train's whistle or its steady clack over a loose section of rail, unless it was a colicky infant or an old man who had given up slumber for smoking. To the residents of these haunts, the train by day was a token of the broader country, trailing their thoughts along behind it as it bore away into the horizon, running beside roads they had never driven, threading towns they had never needed to see because they already lived in one exactly like them. By night, the train was a river through their sleep.

If, during the war, you happened to ride the Southern Pacific railroad, you would likely have seen billboards that stood on right-of-ways throughout its system: "It Takes

8 Tons of Freight to K.O. 1 Jap." After the war, Americans might have found solace in that fact—if only it had remained a fact. At the rate of eight tons of matériel a soul, no country on earth had the power to threaten the United States, for no other country could manufacture military freight in such quantities or muster the transport needed to move it to its ultimate destination. As long as those were the conditions of war, the United States had never been safer in its history. But those were no longer the conditions of war. In 1945 the scientists at Los Alamos compacted the strange forces of the universe into a single weapon, and the freight bill changed. The Little Boy bomb, the atomic device dropped on Hiroshima, weighed 9,700 pounds, 4.85 tons. It killed 140,000 Japanese by the end of 1945. It was not delivered by rail.

Just as you're winning a hand of pinochle, you find you're also losing a game of poker you didn't even know had been dealt. That was the way the war ended for the United States. It didn't matter whether or not Americans thought the atomic bomb should have been dropped. The unimagined consequences of its detonation redounded upon them anyway. On the evening of August 6, 1945, the day Hiroshima was bombed, H. V. Kaltenborn, an NBC radio commentator, told his national audience, "We must assume that with the passage of only a little time, an improved form of the new weapon we use today can be turned against us." On August 12, 1945, three days after the Fat Man was dropped on Nagasaki and two days after Japan indicated its willingness to surrender, Edward R. Murrow said on CBS radio, "Seldom, if ever, has a war ended leaving the victors with such a sense of uncertainty and fear, with such a realization that the future is obscure and that survival is not assured."

The atomic bomb fell on Japan, but it also fell on this country's air of remove. Just when the United States seemed most secure in its geographical isolation, just when its physical immensity had been revealed to more of its citizens than ever before in its history, the bomb ended America's remoteness from war. Out of any sky, an atomic bomb might eventually fall, annihilating distance. Suddenly, America seemed vulnerable not merely to the heightened levels of conventional violence inaugurated in World War II, but also to a new, inconceivable wound. "[One] forgets the effect on Japan," said the New York *Herald Tribune*, "as one senses the foundations of one's own universe trembling." In a just war, the only acceptable pity is self-pity.

The shock waves the United States felt after the bombing of Hiroshima and Nagasaki took the form of bitter paradox, ring after concentric ring of it. To drop the bomb on Japan was to drop it on America. To win by the bomb's means was to risk never winning again. To employ it terminated the only conditions under which it could legitimately be employed. The virtues that war traditionally exposed, the bomb destroyed. It killed private death and made public death impossible too, because it left behind no public. It turned death into a passageless passage. It made fear of living after its holocaust worse than fear of dying. If, like President Truman, one thanked God "that it has come to us instead of to our enemies," one recognized that at a time of dire need God had given the bomb to the Right Country—a nation of just motives and purity of heart. But was that providential argument strengthened or weakened when the Right Country chose to drop it? If the gift was divine, as Truman believed, it was a terrible gift; its use inflamed the conscience mightily.

For to use the bomb was to destroy the enemy in imagination before the enemy could actually be destroyed. Facing a weapon of such sudden, inexplicable terror, such superfluous retribution, any population becomes an innocent population. That was the bomb's most disheartening ambiguity: vulnerability and innocence became hopelessly linked. The utter vulnerability of the Japanese in Hiroshima and Nagasaki during the moments before they were overflown made them innocent, though they were unquestionably the enemy. The image of Hiroshima rising on a bright August Monday morning and going about its business routinely, unknowingly, during the incommensurable forty-three seconds of the bomb's freefall is as penetrating as the image of the ghosting and cindering that followed. And when Americans first understood the completeness of the bomb's devastation, their own vulnerability—so acutely felt because they learned of victory, exposure, and guilt at the same instant—rendered them innocent before the bomb too.

With immense effort, the Manhattan Project had converted a natural mystery, one of those matters on which nature is so tacit, into a set of numbers and diagrams that could be copied as easily as an industrial recipe for cream of mushroom soup. Having secretly solved the mystery, the United States was left to fret openly over keeping the secret. But whose secret was it? Only a tiny corps of Western scientists was permitted to know the bomb in all its technical dimensions. (They also knew that before long the Soviet Union would certainly build a bomb of its own, physical laws being unaffected by politics.) It was an impossible situation. Americans neither understood the details of the weapon they dropped on Hiroshima nor, ultimately, could they keep those details from being divulged. The final paradox of the atomic bomb was that to comprehend its mystery one must also have the power to betray its secret.

Which is deeper, a secret or a mystery? In 1946, Eddie Wenzek attended a welcome-home party for a classmate and swim-team friend from East High School. Eddie's friend was a smart Polish boy who grew up over his parents' grocery in the south part of the city—near the shipping channels and drawbridges and private industrial streets—from which he used to walk to school in central Buffalo. Instead of serving in the armed forces, he wound up at Columbia University as a chemist in the Manhattan Project, where he worked on gas-flow separation factors for metallic membranes and kinetic studies on corrosion. At the party, held in the family apartment over the grocery store, Eddie took his classmate aside and asked what he had done during the war. His friend said, "Eddie, I'll show you." He went to his briefcase and took out an article based on his Manhattan Project research, a text littered with chemical symbols and mathematical notation. Eddie later said, "It was Greek to me."

◆

Strange Forces Hold the Universe Together . . . And Blow It Apart . . . The Atomic Age Has Arrived. There is a pantleg caught in 1947's sock . . . and this is why. The pantleg problem is not a sign of simplicity, as if 1947 were some hayseed year fresh off the country bus or a simple dreamer with indigestion, wearing a pointed nightcap; it is a sign of preoccupation, of learning to live with a truly modern neurosis, of recurrent but ever more familiar anxiety over Joe's libido and his appliance situation, over the financial health of John and Ellen Jones, over the value of television, over a nuclear existence.

And yet the worst anxieties do slowly fade as they become customary. Even as the results of the 1946 Bikini tests make it clear that fallout will broadcast devastation downwind of any blast, you learn that you can take it in stride. In late 1945 the nation's vast spaces shrank to a single city block in one great burst of atomic vulnerability and fear. The United States has since unclenched. America's calendar landscapes, its wooded valleys where snow falls across an inviting view and life is lived as it once was, can again enjoy their serene isolation, knowing they won't be targeted by the Russians. In 1947 you can stand on the roadside looking over the warm hood of your ponderous black De Soto toward one of those blissful pockets of rural life and ask yourself which number better measures the nation's harried innocence: 142 million Americans, 17,000 TV sets, or a total stockpile of 13 atomic bombs?

Once you have imagined the worst that is known and sucked your breath in hard two or three times, you can get back to the getting good of the living going on around you. After a while, all these arguments about bombs and innocence and vulnerability and secrets finally boil down not quite to nothing, but to the atomic concerns they really are: an isotope in the bone, a nervousness on occasion, a hitch in the walk, but not a mortal impairment to the pleasure of life. Not yet. Not here. All this doubt and concern is just a split reed in the clarinet section of a big band that won't stop playing "Stardust" on that account. Nineteen forty-seven is a good year to remodel a bar, add shrimp to a menu, hang a fat and meaty neon sign on a corner in the darkness.

One day 1947 will seem like a long time ago. People of a certain age in that unpredictable future will look back, as if through a tree-shaded succession of unfenced backyards, as if from the gondola of a dirigible up where the air is thin, and see their parents courting in what seem to be unimaginably innocent circumstances, which is exactly what their own children will see when they look back in turn from the twenty-first century.

But to get that far into the future, you must pass 1955, where you will want to stop and admire the domestication of the atom. In that year, a man called Peter Gust was invited to Yucca Flats, Nevada, to witness Operation Cue—the testing of an atomic bomb. Peter Gust, whose real name was Peter Gust Economou, was the nationally famous owner of Buffalo's Park Lane Restaurant, where Eddie and Rene Wenzek held their wedding reception. He was also a former Best Dressed American Restaurateur, a local radio celebrity famous for his bi-weekly five-minute food program called "Your Host, Peter Gust," and a member of the Buffalo Sewer Authority.

At Yucca Flats Peter Gust joined a group of food-service executives who were participating in "the first Civil Defense field exercise to be conducted in connection with a nuclear explosion." Their job was to execute "a vast workable plan for the mass feeding of persons displaced and dispossessed by atomic attack." The April weather was atrocious and the test kept being postponed. During the delay, Peter Gust drove to Las Vegas to catch the act of his old friend Liberace, who used to perform frequently at the Park Lane. It was Peter Gust's famous blue tuxedo that gave Liberace the idea of dressing with a little more flair.

Eventually the weather over southern Nevada cleared. The bomb was detonated just before dawn. It arose from the desert floor in a fireball. As it ascended, it looked at first like a young morel mushroom and then the winds flattened it into a cloud resembling "a drooping morning glory." Survival City, a model town of immaculate innocence inhabited only by a group of dummies called the Darling family, was obliterated with all their worldly belongings. Afterward, in his capacity as caterer to the atomically displaced and dispossessed, Peter Gust served a breakfast of Philadelphia Scrapple for one thousand.

THE FALLS

*In that long—long time, never still for a single
moment. Never dried, never froze, never slept,
never rested.*

Abraham Lincoln

In 1953, George Ditzel—the George of George & Eddie's,
a tall, handsome man with blond hair and a long chin—
sold his piece of the business to Eddie Wenzek, bought
back into a retail dairy with five routes, and moved out
of the front apartment above the bar to the suburbs. George
took his wife, Jean (née Wenzek), his golf stroke, his Buick
convertible, and his two children, and settled into a beautiful stone and pale brick house on a curving street in
Cheektowaga, on the edge of the more sumptuous community of Amherst. The house was a dream. It had a
knotty-pine basement with a wet bar and a Ping-Pong

table. It had velvety-painted interior walls and a flagstone porch and a patio. It had a colonial kitchen. There was space in the master bedroom for a full-sized vanity and space on the sideboard to display all of the cups and the punchbowl that Freda Wenzek had given her daughter. There was a closet in every bedroom. Through every window streamed daylight dappled with reflections from the grass and from the flower beds where Jean and George spent much of their time. The Grover Cleveland Golf Course was only a few blocks away.

Every Sunday Jean and George stopped by 722 Sycamore Street on their way home from the church they attended near Humboldt Parkway. Every Friday they returned to eat fish fry. They sat at the bar and had drinks with Eddie and Renee. They visited with Tom in the bar and with Freda upstairs and said hello to friends having dinner in the backroom. Then they got in the convertible and drove home to Hunting Road on one of the new expressways that led to the city's edge. In the suburbs, quiet lay on the lawns like an invisible snowfall. Every house was a beauty, an island afloat in an emerald sea. Their own house seemed particularly gorgeous. It was a miracle how new the driveway looked, how wide the windows opened, how fresh the air smelled. It was also a miracle how soon the old neighborhood at Sycamore and Herman came to seem old.

But down in the old neighborhood, on the East Side of Buffalo, the world continued to shuck itself at the failure of light every evening. The years passed more quickly than anyone had ever dreamed possible. Eddie Wenzek and his bride moved into the front apartment above the bar, which Renee decorated with the advice of a downtown department store. The accent was on lightness and newness. There were scalloped moldings and knotty-pine wainscoting left from the Ditzels' years there (Jean adored knotty pine). For the kitchen Renee chose a wallpaper with country flair—roosters and barns and ears of corn. Ceramic dogs and chunks of Hawaiian coral lined the living-room bookshelves. The armchairs were armless. The coffee table and matching desk were made of blond wood with black iron drawer pulls. On the end tables stood lamps in the shape of dancers: a man wearing green tights and a black vest, a woman wearing a green skirt and black bodice. Both lamps had black shades and furry trim.

And downstairs? The bar scarcely aged, except in the eyes of those who had moved to the suburbs. In 1947 Eddie Wenzek and George Ditzel had thrown their grand opening party with a sense of almost intolerable excitement. Everything but the hangovers had been new. And now, just like that, George & Eddie's had served drinks and dinner for a thousand nights running, then two thousand, then three thousand, and soon there were two little girls, Eddie's daughters, Cindy and Reggie, riding tricycles the length of the restaurant in the still morning hours when only a few men were tippling on stools at the bar. One minute Eddie was polishing a maroon 1949 Cadillac. Then he was pulling a blue-and-white '54 Olds 98 out of the heated garage. Before long he was honking for Renee and the girls in a black '57 Olds 98 with red stripes and three carburetors. Time was a revelation.

But time had been set aside in the suburbs. All the houses had been built at once, and everyone had moved in together, so no one aged except in respect to the nonsuburban world. When George and Jean drove down to the East Side after a few months in their new house, they saw things they had never really laid eyes on before, though they had lived on the East Side for all of their lives. Seven twenty-two Sycamore Street was a palimpsest, a building on which generation after generation, including their own, had left its mark. It had dominated the corner of Sycamore and

Herman since the late nineteenth century. How many owners had there been in that time? Three men—Frank Lauk, Jacob Bystiak, and John Buclaw—had owned it just in the seven years before Thomas Wenzek bought it in 1922. How large were their families and how many strangers had roomed upstairs? No one knows. What were the building's original outlines? Lost, probably not for the first time, in the expansion of 1933. The oldest parts of the building bore directly on the newest.

Over the last hundred years nearly every wave of immigrants to reach Buffalo—Jews, Germans, Poles, and now blacks—had swept through the East Side, reworking it to their needs until they had saved enough money to move to more middle-class sections of town. For every corner business that had prospered and grown stalwart— every Thomas Wenzek Restaurant, every George & Eddie's—another dozen had failed. The oldest blocks were entirely piecemeal, their rows of houses telescoped, patched, and reporched until they looked nothing alike. There were no wholly new blocks, just new houses where old ones had been pulled down or burned, houses with a deeper or shallower setback than the rest of the block or a different alignment to the curb. It was a jumble of eras, decade heaped upon century, a temporal fabric shored up and plastered by years and months, while on the rooftops weathervanes twitched in every breath of the wind.

And it was the same with people on the East Side, a jumble of ages and kinds. Schoolgirls in white blouses and blue jumpers ended their Friday-morning communion fast with jelly doughnuts and cartons of milk from Zwack's Delicatessen. They crossed Genesee Street holding hands two by two as Black and Brown Franciscan nuns from St. Mary of Sorrows kept watch. During the sacrament the girls knelt beside women of pious character, women who, had it not been for husbands with ruddy temperaments and firm holds on life, would have bound themselves fast by the three knots the nuns wore at the ends of their rope belts, one knot for each of their vows. Those women needed no suburbs. They needed a pew and the Broadway Market. In the pew you could study the delicate lineaments of the crucified Christ and in the market see what it means for the word to become flesh. The people there, and all across the East Side, were as varied as the produce on display in tilted-up boxes and crates: eggplants, onions, tomatoes, radishes, potatoes, turnips, beets, a Turk's-turban squash every now and then. Where had they all come from, these types yet unseen on the still, curving streets of the suburbs?

And the variety had only grown since the war. For where there had once been scarcely a black man or woman in Buffalo—there were only forty-five hundred when Eddie Wenzek was born—they numbered now in the many tens of thousands. They had begun arriving from the South just as Buffalo's heavy industry, where every other mi-grating generation had found work and the means to rise in the world, started to shut down after the war, to shut down and then to collapse. Like the Polish immigrants before them, Buffalo's black people came to (and were pushed toward) the only neighborhood they could afford, the East Side, especially the Humboldt Park area and near Jefferson Avenue, eight blocks west of George & Eddie's. When Poles had first settled in East Buffalo, they had faced the shopkeeping, beer-brewing pride—and an ancient hos-tility to Slavs—of the Germans who had come there before them. Between the Poles and the blacks there was even less sympathy. Like many whites in the city, the residents of the East Side, who themselves had been described by Woodrow Wilson as their country's "sordid and hapless elements," "men out of the ranks where there was neither skill nor energy nor any initiative of quick intelligence," now looked on their black neighbors with similar feelings.

On the major streets radiating outward from the lake through East Buffalo, on Broadway and Sycamore and Genesee, "For Rent" signs began to appear only in Polish, and they went longer and longer unanswered. Stores sat vacant, their windows soaped and then boarded. If by chance it had been some time since you last drove in from the suburbs, you might assume, if only from the tone of the conversations you overheard among white shopkeepers and shoppers alike, that some miserable weather was expected to blow off the lake before long. When you got home you would cover the patio furniture and set out the houseplants that needed a soaking and then be surprised when the rains never came.

But whatever the future holds, time has to pass before it arrives, and who knows what time will bring? Every morning saw Renee in the restaurant kitchen, every evening found Eddie behind the bar. Sometimes Eddie and Renee went dancing with their friends in the clubs that retained a sophisticated flavor—the Peter Stuyvesant Room, where they foxtrotted on a backlit glass mosaic depicting that Dutchman's arrival in the New World—or Chez Ami, where early one morning Eddie did the cha-cha on an empty dance floor with the wife of a local funeral-home owner. One year Eddie ran a fried-shrimp tent at the Erie County Fair—the first person ever to serve shrimp there. He was dismayed when the truck conveying the bingo concession ran over his tent, but he was more dismayed when fairgoers bought mostly French fries.

Then came the Christmas party held at George & Eddie's for the priests of the Minor Seminary. It was snowing like mad. You couldn't see across the street. Light from the windows poured out onto the snow-covered walks and onto the untraveled roadway beyond. The bar was crowded with clean-shaven young and old men dressed in black, a few parishioners, and women of pious character or women who at any rate were fond of priests. Renee's food was superb. Eddie was unstinting with cheer. A window dresser from Sears had decorated the backbar; red ribbons spiraled up the marble columns; evergreen boughs overhung them; ornaments of gold and silver dangled in the mirror.

The air filled with the coughing of chain smokers and the chesty laughter of men whose religion had tempered none of their appetites. (But in the backbar mirror between the marble columns and the regal decorations, it looked like a conclave of Renaissance popes.) When twelve o'clock came, Renee said goodnight and began to walk up the family stairs. Every priest in the room turned and sang as one voice in many parts the popular hit "Goodnight, Irene." The children, awake alone in the light of a snow-lit sky, heard the singing from their beds directly above. Their grandparents were already fast asleep.

◆

Freda Wenzek died after settling with a frail sigh, her weak heart gone, into a chair from which her son and her husband were powerless to raise her. It was the flesh that took Freda, and each damp spadeful of earth that rattled on her coffin was a weight lifted from her chest, until in the end her spirit rose as easily in death as if it were a particle of goose down rising on a warm current of lamplight as she finished another feather bed for another one of her children. On the day she died in 1957, one of the priests who patronized George & Eddie's climbed the private stairs to the back apartment in the canary building with the red roof and bade Freda Wenzek farewell from this world and so welcome to the next.

In her absence, Thomas Wenzek, his hair grown the color of frozen, salted February asphalt, lived more and more downstairs, in the hubbub of the bar. And yet as time passed, the back apartment—a rambling set of rooms with floral curtains and stout velvet furniture, an ornamental fireplace, Persian rugs, and an archway, icons and statues, chandeliers and shell sconces of translucent pink glass, a heavy rocking chair in the kitchen, a bathroom adorned by the same aquatic frescoes the bar had once featured—came inevitably to seem fuller of Tom and emptier of Freda, though now and then Tom caught a reminiscence of her scent, as pleasing and as wholly of place as that of the cedar closet in Freda's bedroom or the attic, where she had stored barrels full of linen and broken china. The rest of the apartment began to smell of Liederkranz cheese, a dark and dated odor. The apartment's furnishings and its lone inhabitant dragged those rooms back in time while daily the whole external world updated itself, to everyone's complete surprise.

Tom grew closer to his sister, Julia. Instead of taking his homemade sausages to be smoked at the Wardynski sausage plant near St. Stanislaus Church, he drove to Julia's house on Weaver Street, down near the shrunken railroads, not far from the old Black Diamond Bar. In the backyard Julia kept a fifty-five-gallon oil drum she had turned into a smoker. It was she, if the truth be known, who was the better butcher in that family, for she was less given to grand gestures than her brother and she had worked longer on the farm. Together Julia and Tom hung sausages, those pale clinging false intestines, over a broomstick and kindled a cool, hardwood fire at the base of the drum.

And in return, Julia and her husband, Frank, now retired

and without a bar of their own anymore, began to frequent George & Eddie's regularly, going downtown to join Tom at the front window table where, except for his annual Florida vacation, he had sat for a part of each day now going on forty years. Julia Pajonk had become a woman of indeterminate age, with wicker-colored hair and thick, strong arms, as if she had remained an agriculturist after all. She had never withered like her mother in Poland, nor had her face become a bony cross, even when mantled under a babushka. If anything, the darkness that had shrouded Julia's eyes during her middle years had lifted as she grew older. The lenses of her rimless glasses refracted additional light onto her face, so that if you saw her at a first communion outside St. Casimir's Church, for instance—watching a neighbor child in a white dress march beneath the crossed swords of the Knights of Columbus, who stood erect in cockades and plumes—or at an afternoon birthday party in the dining room of George & Eddie's, where a doll cake was being served to a band of excited little girls, Eddie's daughters and their friends —you would never guess that Julia Pajonk was called by many who knew her "The General."

When Sunday afternoons came, she and Tom drove alone in his car down the Erie coast, stopping in saloons along Lake Shore Road, pausing here and there to look at the slag heaps in Lackawanna, where the steel mills were breathing their last, or to stand on the Barcelona bluffs and wonder why Canada got the sand and the U.S. the rocks. They watched the ice arrive on Lake Erie in winter and go out again in spring; they saw houses arise on improbable lots and disappear after raking storms.

No one knows what Tom and Julia talked about, of course. It may have been gossip about East Side friends and businesses dead and gone, talk about how the neighborhood was changing. They may have done nothing more than read road signs and billboards to each other. But there is such a thing as inference. And of Tom Wenzek and his sister, Julia Pajonk, a pair of aging immigrants with no destination but suppertime, the blacktop resounding beneath the tires like a quartet of muted horns, one would like to infer a conversational visit, perhaps only by means of the most glancing allusions, to the Galician river valley where Piwniczna lay, beeches and firs blurring the hilltops, the Poprad glimmering in and out of the shadows in a scene set an ocean, two wars, and another lifetime ago. And how could such long Sunday drives escape without the awareness dawning upon brother and sister that time had carried them farther than any immigrant ship had ever done, that time itself was the immigrant ship? The past had accrued in shocking amounts. One grew old in the moment it took to remember youth.

Sometimes instead of turning south, Tom turned north and then west, following the River Road as it bent its route toward Niagara Falls. On this drive too he and Julia stopped for drinks, perhaps at a marina bar in sight of the chemical plants and the tire factories and the world-famous lumberyards of Tonawanda, or at a tavern just downstream of Cayuga Island, a small logjam of houses separated from the mainland by the Little Niagara River, houses whose lawns ran right down to the big Niagara, swirling and siphoning its way along the island's edge, from time to time sucking a chunk of sod into the flow, where it quickly dissolved in the turbulence, leaving only a scalp of grass afloat on the current until that too finally sank out of sight. Almost anywhere along the River Road, Tom and Julia could have seen the mosaic domes on the synagogues of the city of Ararat shimmering across the river, had that city of refuge ever been built. Instead, they watched the bland banks of Grand Island slide along the far side of the Tonawanda Channel, low trees and willows overhanging the water and darkening it with shadows. Sailboats toyed in the broad river, always nervous of the reaches below Navy Island, where mist billowed up from the Falls. Powerboats like the one Eddie Wenzek owned in the early Fifties, the *Ree Nee*, blatted rudely upstream, crisscrossing wakes. Oil refineries soured the air and adulterated the landscape. High-tension power lines towered suddenly aloft from step-up transformers and looped away southward into the distance. And in parking lots on both sides of Niagara Falls the curious gathered, those who had dreamed of this sight for years as well as those, like Tom and Julia, for whom it had been a toss-up: take another peek over the precipice or get home early, in time for a nap.

In the bitter autumn of 1678 Father Hennepin, afoot with the La Salle expedition on the downstream western heights, first witnessed Niagara Falls. "On his left sank the cliffs, the furious river raging below," wrote Francis Parkman, the nineteenth-century historian, "till at length, in primeval solitudes unprofaned as yet by the pettiness of man, the imperial cataract burst upon his sight." But the only primeval solitudes any longer to be found at the Falls were those concealed in the breasts of tourists. All across western New York State, highways beetled toward the Falls. On their flanks sprang up motels, and beside the motels, information booths. Niagara had become a paradox: an international monument almost totally obscured by hints of its location.

For more than a century and a half after Hennepin saw the Falls, language had been unequal to the sight, for the sublime requires an admixture of terror. But in the twentieth century, itself so attuned to the sublimity of pure terror, Niagara Falls became utterly equal to everyday language, demoted to the demotic, so to speak. "Niagara Falls Information!" the booths proclaimed, as if tourists came hungry for solid knowledge, could not do without it for more than a block or two, their rapacity such that it took a whole county of reference desks to supply it. But of the single piece of information that everyone truly desired there was never any mention made: how would it feel to go over the Falls unaided by even so much as a barrel? In the twentieth century the vista no longer matters, only the vertigo.

The Buffalo story, the one you overhear in barbershops and beauty parlors and corner saloons, among businessmen lunching at the Lafayette Hotel and at meetings of Elks and Shriners and Red Men, is secretly a story about the Falls, for Buffalo was built upstream of a timeless catastrophe that is "never still," as Abraham Lincoln said, "for a single moment." You could be fishing off the Black Rock Canal and fall into the current, right off town, and the river would carry you downstream under the bridges, past Strawberry Island, Motor Island, Tonawanda Island, Cayuga Island, Grand Island, Navy Island, Dufferin Island, Three Sisters Islands, Brother Island, Goat Island, and so out of reach of all mankind.

When Eddie Wenzek pours you a drink and starts a tale, you know you are about to listen to the saga of some man who, morally speaking, was walking north along Niagara Street one day, took a misstep to the left, landed in the river and was borne into oblivion. Buffalo, Tonawanda, Amherst, Cheektowaga, it's all the same. The guy had a nice car (a Buick, a Cadillac, a Packard, an Olds). He had a beautiful wife with a lovely figure (the word "figure" never resolving itself into constituent parts, not in Eddie's conversation). He had a couple of nice kids, a good job, and always plenty of cash in pocket, a roll as big as your fist. He had everything the Niagara Frontier could offer. But one day a misstep occurred in his life. It might have been sin or a trick of fate. And he was swept right over the Falls. He lost it all, and then he died. It was a nice funeral, lots of the old crowd on hand. Eddie was a pall-bearer again and again, a sign of the wideness of his acquaintance and the esteem in which bar owners were held on the East Side.

"Now this was an ideal family," says Eddie, and right away you can tell what's coming. This was a man, a retail jeweler, with two kids, a lovely wife, and a Lincoln Continental. Whenever he came into George & Eddie's, he ordered a cigar, a Gold Star Havana, three for a dollar. During a routine visit to the doctor he found he had cancer. Before long he was taken to the hospital to finish out his days. Eddie brought him his favorite cigar, which the jeweler ran under his nose with pleasure and set carefully on the nightstand. "It was like I gave him a diamond ring," Eddie says, "which of course he had many of."

Take the monsignor who fell into the Niagara Gorge during a spiritual retreat. Or Eddie's friend whose real-estate license came in the mail on the day he died. Or consider the fellow who ran a tavern called "Bob's Castaway" ("Bob was the guy's name"). The moral turns, as always, on the loss of assets, the going over the Falls from what had seemed a good life. "This guy had a Chrysler Imperial, looked like a limousine; of course they all looked like limousines in those days." Bob sold mutual funds while tending bar. But he was also a Casanova. "The husband came home," Eddie says, "caught the two of them, and shot the gashhound. Dead."

Or imagine the case of the high-born Polish émigré. This was a man of aristocratic birth, raised in Europe, a son of culture, a violinist in the Buffalo Philharmonic. (And as Eddie says, "When you're philharmonic anything, you're the best.") To make a buck he took a job distributing second-rate liquor, which Eddie, who usually bought only the top-drawer stuff, purchased now and again out of simple charity. His fatal weaknesses were women and the horses. One day, the disparity of it all overwhelmed him and he drove his car into the water at the Buffalo Yacht Club. They pulled his body out before it went over the Falls—at the foot of the pier, as a matter of fact—but the principle remains the same.

Look at that half mile of water slipping over the curve at the brink of the Horseshoe Falls, the same curve as the top line on a 1947 refrigerator. Imagine yourself falling with it, half submerged at the point on the crest where the water turns luminous green from the sudden flush of light suffusing it. In winter, when the sky is tucked in close to the ground and the spray freezes in shafts on the walls of the Gorge, the fear of going over the Falls is no worse than the fear of getting wet. But in summer the thought makes you turn away from the spectacle before you, Niagara thundering in your ears, that great slab of water sliding eerily, greasily toward the edge of the Lockport dolostone that caps the Falls, branches and boughs dipping and bobbing in the flow, almost comically indifferent to their fate in the instant they vanish. If you went over, you would inevitably see some odd and poignant detail—a seagull preening on an exposed rock in the rapids—just as you fell away. You would fail to hear yourself screaming. You might drown in the vapor as you tumbled. Instead of floating outward like a jet of mist, you would be forced downward by a massive column of water. You would be flattened by the roar. You would be crushed from above, ground into the talus, held down, twisted, eddied, until by chance you (no longer you, a leg, an arm, a head) caught an updraft and surfaced again, only to lodge in some place remote from rescue (if rescue is the word), buried in open air, exhumed when the mist lifted for a second, then buried again from sight.

It's a potent story. It's a wonder Buffalo doesn't hurl

one average citizen over the Falls each year, by public acclamation, just to reinforce the point. Play carefully around water. Walk upright, make no missteps. Wash the Olds every weekend and have the agency mechanic tune it often. Tire pressure is important. Stay off the booze. And the broads.

After one of those long Sunday drives, sometime in the early Sixties, Thomas Wenzek found it hard to eat. His appetite left him. He was just not hungry, he said. Renee took over the care of her father-in-law, and for a period he seemed to improve. At the hospital, the diagnosis was bowel cancer. A young surgeon sketched for Eddie a diagram of Thomas Wenzek's intestines on a cafeteria napkin, showing what he planned to cut away and how he intended to resection. To Eddie, in private, the surgeon gave his father two years to live. Then he sent them home. What do you do with the napkin on which a stranger has drawn the bowels of your dying father?

When he had retired in 1947, his friends and his family had asked Tom why he and Freda didn't move to the suburbs. Why not buy a small house where he could expand his rose garden and enjoy some peace? Tom was not the kind of man who explained himself. Soon the question began to make him angry. He didn't want a private place, Tom finally answered; he wanted to see his friends. Everyone stopped asking. Tom sat at his window table and played cards and drank and watched Sycamore Street, though much of what he saw on the sidewalk he disliked. It made him wish for old times back.

There had been a custom among saloonkeepers like Tom, a custom which George and Eddie allowed to lapse when they took over the bar. Every couple of weeks in those days long past, a saloonkeeper would take a night off from his work and make a round of every saloon in the area. At each bar he visited, he stood drinks for the house, to prime the pump, so to speak. It was a picture to remember, those bartenders wandering the streets of East Buffalo in turn, night after night, dropping in at nearly every corner for another shot, thawing their feet on the fender of a coal stove, warming their lungs on the moist barroom air, visiting with friends. If you worked it right, you'd end your circuit only a corner away from home and bed. Practically every night of the year one saloonkeeper or another walked into the Thomas Wenzek Restaurant and told Tom to set 'em up. That had been society. That had been reciprocation. That and the many evenings when Freda and her four sisters and their girlish mother Anastasya sat at the bar drinking Pink Ladies, taking turns on the dance floor. How they could dance! How they could drink Pink Ladies! They kept Tom busy with the egg whites and the gin. Why would anyone ever want to leave?

After the operation to resect Tom's bowel, Eddie took his father to stay at George and Jean's house in Cheektowaga, where there were fewer distractions. The next night Tom asked Eddie to come get him. Eddie told him to rest up and feel better. Tom called several times the next day, wanting to come home. Eddie drove out to Hunting Road to pick up his father. When they pulled into the driveway on Herman Street, Tom got out of the car, marched in the family entrance, set his suitcase under the stairs, and walked directly to his table under the front window of the bar.

A year later, Tom returned from his Florida vacation with a peculiarly yellow tan, which was no tan at all but a sign that the cancer afflicting his bowel had invaded his liver. The doctors declared it inoperable. Tom began to drink Ovaltine made with cream. After a while, he let no one feed him but his nine-year-old granddaughter Reggie, who lived across the hall and whom Tom had taught to like calf brains with bacon in scrambled eggs. Then one Thursday in early October 1965, about the hour of day when Tom was accustomed to have breakfast, Reggie came downstairs to tell her father, who was working the lunch rush behind the bar, that she thought her grandfather was dead. She was right.

Eddie wept. The priests from Transfiguration and St. Mary of Sorrows arrived together. Okoniewski and Son handled the funeral arrangements. Eddie asked Mr. Okoniewski to turn off the mournful background music in the funeral parlor. Everyone was far too sad already. "That's enough now," said George to Jean, who had gone to pieces. A funeral mass was said at Transfiguration Church at 10 A.M. Monday morning. Thomas Wenzek was buried beside Freda in St. Stanislaus Cemetery. Their graves are covered with pachysandra. They are surrounded by friends and neighbors. The survivors drove back to George & Eddie's. Everyone said that the best thing for Eddie was to get right back to work. So Eddie opened the bar and everyone started to drink. "A Catholic funeral," said Renee. "You really know you're dead when it's over."

Julia Pajonk survived her brother by eight months. At her funeral, the left side of her face appeared to be slipping toward her feet, a sign of the stroke that killed her. Lying in a coffin with its hatch flung open, Julia seemed well tucked in for the long wait ahead, her glasses seated firmly on the bridge of her nose, a little higher perhaps than when she'd been up and walking. Her broad shoulders were squared by the coffin's overstuffed satin lining, her interlocked hands clutched a rosary, and a windbreak of red and·white flowers bent over the casket. If you lifted a camera to your eye, as her daughter did, and took a last snapshot of the mortal remains of Julia Pajonk, being careful to stand far enough back to frame all the blossoms in the viewfinder, Julia would appear sadly diminished by the trick of the lens, discernible only as an artificial blush hidden among flowers that cast their scent across the room, scent that lurked in everyone's nostrils till displaced by the pungent odors of the funeral breakfast.

From St. Casimir's Roman Catholic Church, Julia Pajonk's body was driven several miles north to St. Stanislaus Cemetery and interred on a morning in early June 1966, not far from Thomas and Freda. And yet it seems natural to think of Julia being borne to her resting place not, as Tom was, in a low-slung Cadillac hearse, smoothing through intersections, past burger joints and muffler shops, but in another manner, the way it is done in Piwniczna, Poland, where she and her brother were born and raised.

The graveyard in Piwniczna isn't nocked into a corner of I-90 and the Kensington Expressway. You never feel that if it weren't a cemetery it might be an industrial park or a housing tract or a shopping mall anchored by a Sears at one end and a Sibley's at the other. If, in Piwniczna, the cemetery didn't happen to be hallowed ground, it might be a horse pasture or a field of barley. There the coffin is plain wood. Its lid rises into a high-pitched gable like the roof of a house, and it is hung in lace with the pallor of a snowfall barely whitening the ground early in winter's first storm. Pallbearers step solemnly out of the church and over the Poprad River bridge, their arms forming a lattice beneath the casket, hands clasping each other's shoulders. Priests in white surplices precede them, the mourners trailing behind. In the near distance, hills lift away from the river valley and into the clouds, and on a gravel bed a thin, dark line of steel rails can be seen running parallel to the Poprad. A light drizzle falls over all the region.

But one is buried from the life one inhabits.

Thomas Wenzek lived on in his wishes. His daughters cleaned out the cupboards, as they had cleaned out their

mother's closets nearly a decade before. One of the waitresses received a bedroom set. Renee gave the remaining
furniture, except a few odds and ends, including the bed
in which Freda was laid out at her death, to the nuns at
the Minor Seminary, where its stoutness was highly val-
ued. Renee redecorated the back apartment. The accent
was on the expunging of Thomas Wenzek's formidable
presence. She removed the ornamental fireplace and filled
in the windows that opened onto the deck on top of the
garage. The icons and sacred statues disappeared. The photographs and the penny gravure of the Austrian imperial
family went to the attic, where they were stored in the
steamer trunk Thomas had brought with him from the
Old World.

   Everyone thought Eddie would sell out and move to the
suburbs after his father's death, for the neighborhood was
rapidly turning wholly black and the air had filled with
invidiousness between the races. They were wrong. He
was his father's, and his mother's, son. Except for three
years in the service, Eddie had never lived farther from his
parents than across a narrow hallway. He had lived at 722
Sycamore Street since he was two years old. He had always
lived upstairs from his work. And even as the neighborhood changed, as the city and its realtors ghettoized the
East Side, as the streets just downtown from the bar filled
with angrier and angrier black people, as more and more
Poles left for Cheektowaga, business at George & Eddie's
improved. Weekends the place was jammed with old East
Siders who drove in for a top-shelf meal and a couple of
drinks. But only weekends. Eddie began to close Tues-
days. Good bartenders got hard to find; the others were
all drunks. Eddie kept a pistol behind the bar; he had a
license to wear it when making bank deposits. He could
feel the pistol on his heart.

   One June night in 1967, less than two years after his

father's death, Eddie sent Renee and the girls to see George and Jean in Cheektowaga, while he stayed behind at 722 Sycamore Street. The sign outside and the lights in the bar had been turned off so that Eddie could watch the street. He was not pouring after-hours drinks for a few nameless friends. A disturbance had begun further downtown, and for two nights it had fanned outward through the East Side, the streets full of young blacks rioting (though the police hesitated to use that word) in protest over bad housing and lack of jobs, as they had in Detroit and Los Angeles and Newark that year. Sirens could be heard in the distance, and the occasional bark of scatterguns. Cars were overturned, hundreds of young black men and women arrested, and dozens admitted to local emergency rooms with shotgun wounds. The police ordered all local merchants to close their stores and restaurants.

Eddie sat behind the bar with a twenty-two-caliber target rifle in his hands, waiting for the corner door to be flung open by a rioter. He planned to get one, if he had to. He planned to keep his bar, his father's bar, from being burnt to the ground, the fire fueled by his own liquor. Every light in the window of the bar seemed like a sign of arson outside. Finally, the Twelfth Precinct Captain knocked at the door of George & Eddie's. "What the hell are you doing, Eddie?" he said. "I thought I told you to get out of here." And then he informed Eddie that the neighborhood was quiet again, and that he could put down his rifle and turn on the lights, or, better yet, call his wife and turn in.

It took another three years to convince Eddie to sell the bar, and when he did so, the price was a fraction of the business's former value. The buyer was named Bill Harris, a young black man with a loan from the Small Business Administration. Renee was so jubilant that she gave all her hats to Bill Harris's mother. When it was sold, the bar

contained five tables, seventeen chairs, and fourteen stools
in the front room, plus a cash register, an Osterizer, and
an electric steam table. In the kitchen there were a Garland
stove and grill, a U.S. Slicer, a G.E. refrigerator and
freezer, a sixty-pound deep fryer, a Hotel Steak Broiler, a
toaster, three fire extinguishers, and all the dinner plates,
banquet service, and utensils. In the dining room, there
were twenty-two tables, seventy-two chairs, one jukebox,
one bandstand, and one black spinet piano. In the cellar,
Bill Harris found one beer precooler, one walk-in freezer,
one sump pump, one hot-water tank, one incinerator, and
the gas furnace that a steamfitter named Graf had installed
so many years ago.

And soon, before anyone had time to think, May 1970
had come and it was the very last night that George &
Eddie's would ever be open. Eddie took inventory of his
liquor stock and told all his regular customers that for two
bucks a head they could drink as much as they wanted,
until the open bottles were empty, for the unopened bottles
belonged to the new owner. Renee went to bed early.
Many friends stopped to say goodbye. Al and Sis Huetter.
Frank and Mary Heller. Mrs. Mayer, whose husband,
Curly, had been killed in a holdup at his very own Savings
& Loan. Bunny and Ray Pijanowski came. Bunny and Ray
ran a family-owned soft-drinks business in Sloan. They
bottled and distributed the Visniak brand (*visniak* means
"cherry" in Polish). The business would never have gotten
off the ground if Julia Pajonk hadn't given Ray's dad a
loan in the old days. Julia never once paid for Visniak
beverages as long as she ran the Black Diamond Bar.

Two more couples came through the corner door. One
of the men ran an auto-glass business; the other worked
at a shock-absorber factory. The tall blonde woman was
a housewife. The other, short and graying, was a piano
teacher and ham radio operator. They all shared a duplex.

Eddie took their photo. They faced the lens, casually arranged. Tall, short, man, woman, they mixed easily together, slipping into an unthinking, disorganized pose. Behind them, running at an angle toward the viewer out the right side of the frame, the backbar mirror crosses the picture almost surreptitiously. It alters their postures. In the camera's viewfinder, Eddie has posed the couples with a waving hand. But in the mirror they have been transformed. Light catches their left cheekbones and turns their randomness into quiet perfection. The reflection is the work of a painter at the last of many sittings, when the models know their job and the artist is poised to recognize the touch that ends his labors. In the mirror, those four look like a quartet of angels just beginning their descant above the whole human choir. For a moment. Then the flash goes off and they turn separately to the bar—two couples who have aged week by week, year by year in this restaurant. They order a Manhattan, a straight whiskey, and a couple of Old-Fashioneds.

Eddie stayed up late that night. He saw the last customer, the last old friend, out the door at 4 A.M. He turned out the lights and locked the corner door behind him. Then, while Renee and the girls slept, he backed his '66 Buick Electra out of its heated garage and drove down to Front Park, under the Buffalo approach to the Peace Bridge. There, for the first time in his entire life, he watched the sun come up on the waters of Lake Erie where they spill into the Niagara River and stream northward to the Falls.

The Wenzeks moved to the suburbs. They kept a couple of bar stools and some schupers as mementos. As a housewarming present, Frank Pajonk, Julia's husband, gave them one of the violins he had made during idle hours at the blind pig that Thomas Wenzek had once owned. Friends came by for drinks in the new house and sat stiffly in the den. Eddie and Renee had considered several modest but beautiful houses in Amherst and Williamsville. In a development called Cayuga Heights they found what they were looking for, a split-level ranch with a closet in every bedroom. The builder lived next door. The house had never been occupied. Renee planned to take up gardening. The lot had no grass, no trees, no flowers, and no hedges. The backyard looked like a field grown wild. At its farthest edge there was a chain-link fence and a sharp grassy incline. That incline was the shoulder of the New York State Thruway, just where it widened for the Williamsville toll booth, just where trucks geared down as they came into Buffalo and geared up as they pulled away. That was why Eddie and Renee chose this house. No one would ever build behind them.

After the Wenzeks left the East Side, Bill Harris removed the fat and meaty burgundy sign from the corner of the canary-colored building where it had hung for twenty-three years. In its place he raised a white wooden sign with black lettering. "George & Eddie's" was now "The Scorpion."

Under that name the bar stayed open for another year and a half. The Simon Brewery was no longer in business. Goodwill men no longer existed. Blue pike were nearly extinct. All of Buffalo's elm trees had died long before. Bankruptcy followed at The Scorpion. There were no buyers. The building was abandoned. Soon its windows were broken out and boarded up. Someone worked a hole through the garage door and then through the back wall. Neighborhood kids smoked dope in the old liquor storeroom, a room that had been Eddie's—and before him, his father's—office, a place once full of the delightful smell of wooden liquor cases. Several small fires were started inside. The building was condemned.

A friend at City Hall called Eddie in Williamsville. The

night before the bar was due to be demolished, Eddie drove down to the old neighborhood. He parked on Herman Street. With an old set of keys, he let himself into the building and stepped through the rubble, through the broken glass and the charred papers and the new, confusing smells. He walked into the barroom itself, where the damage was not nearly so bad. There was no saving the backbar mirror, which for nearly half a century had recorded the look of every face that entered the Thomas Wenzek Restaurant and George & Eddie's. On its surface Eddie saw the look of his own face, so unfamiliar amid these ruins. It was as if every one of his former patrons were watching him through the window of the mirror, all nodding in approval, some peering from behind the marble columns. Thomas Wenzek had obtained those columns from a Buffalo gentlemen's club that went out of business just before Prohibition. They had stood on the spot for fifty years. Eddie removed all four of them. He wrapped them in blankets, carried them to the trunk of his car, and drove home to Williamsville.

The next morning Eddie returned to the corner of Sycamore and Herman. He watched the city do its work. A crowd gathered. It cheered every time there was an especially loud crash. When the day ended, 722 Sycamore Street stood no more. Eddie Wenzek drove home to a private place in the suburbs.

EPILOGUE

The trees have grown in around the house in the suburbs now, and the grass is thick underfoot. Maples run in a line across the yard, their trunks ringed by impatiens. Cherry trees, apples, and an Italian plum hang with fruit. Along the low wire fence on the west, Renee has planted tomatoes, raspberries, geraniums, and lilies. To the east, there is a thick and neatly trimmed hedge. Leaning against the chain-link fence that marks the beginning of the state's right-of-way, two bright orange signs say, "Retired? Retiring? Live in Florida!" They face the kitchen window.

Eddie and a guest sit in the midsummer dusk on lawn

chairs at the edge of the patio. They drink beer and watch
the traffic go by on the New York State Thruway. The
near lanes are inbound. They descend from an overpass
only a few hundred yards away, just up the block. On
holiday weekends, traffic backs up well east of the Williamsville toll booth. A driver stuck in the homecoming
rush could look out his passenger-side window, through
the boughs of the fruit trees, to where Eddie and his guest
sit talking against the backdrop of a white clapboard house.
But this evening the traffic moves rapidly—mini-vans,
pickup trucks, recreational vehicles, semis of every variety.
Now and again, a sailboat powers by, bound for Grand
Island or the Erie Marina, where the sunset glistens along
the lake.

On a good day the Thruway sounds like a strong wind
from Syracuse, a wind blowing trade into town. Among
the drivers climbing the gears down in those Kenworth
and Mack and Peterbilt cabs may be young men and
women whom Eddie recruited for truck-driving school.
It is one of the many jobs he has held since he sold George
& Eddie's. It takes him all over Buffalo, into homes of
every description. It gives him the sense that he is helping
young people who want to get started in life, as well as
those who want to begin life again.

In the last twenty years, Eddie has organized school-
lunch programs, sold office products, energy audits, and
replacement windows. He has sold Florida real estate to
Buffalo residents tired of the climate in the Niagara Frontier. Eddie sells nothing without faith, without first be-
lieving in his product. That is salesmanship, he says. He
works out of the trunk of his Chrysler Fifth Avenue and
out of the basement, where he sits at a small steel desk
surrounded by file cabinets. He has a view of the washer
and dryer and the turf out one window. While Eddie
works, sorting prospects, conducting phone interviews,

the radio plays big-band classics of the Forties or the music of Miss Peggy Lee. The basement walls are hung with photographs of pastel Florida cinder-block homes, the kind Eddie once sold. There is a Seagram's promotional print on the wall, a striped bass swimming through heavy surf, and there are birthday cards from Eddie's daughters and grandchildren. There is an Infant of Prague, papal, benign.

Outside on the patio, the evening seems to rise from the East. The western heavens resist it. There is a lull in the traffic, and for a moment you can hear the silence. It swells into the yard like an abrupt tide. Here in the suburbs the houses and shade trees are well spaced, and there is plenty of sky. There are plenty of stars coming out overhead on this warm moonless night. Here where the Thruway defines the horizon, you feel linked to the region. You feel linked to the nation at large.

But you would not have the same feeling down on the East Side. St. Mary of Sorrows is falling to ruin; pedestrians turn away from its crumbling walls. Blue-clad Madonnas are fenced in all over the old neighborhood. Hundreds of structures have been pulled down or torched. And though government-sponsored housing has been built here and there—handsome brick homes on the suburban model—at many addresses decades will pass before construction ever begins again. One such address is 722 Sycamore Street.

It is a vacant lot now, its surface as level as if it were native prairie. You look at the lot, 36 feet wide by 106 feet deep, and you cannot imagine how George & Eddie's ever fit within its confines. The grass is tangled but lush. Paths crisscross the corner. A hedge hedges nothing, for next door is vacant too. The lot's weedy edges are littered with liquor empties. The liquor store across the corner does a carryout business.

Like many former residents of the Polish East Side, Eddie Wenzek feels that he still retains spiritual title to the property. He is wrong. Seven twenty-two Sycamore Street looks like a patch where the very idea of property has been voided. Its vacancy is the sign of something larger than deeds. It resembles a Midwestern field where the stand of crops shows odd variations: the sign of a buried well or a bulldozed farmhouse or soil where there once grew a border of crabapple trees. This lot was Indian territory. It was part of the Great Northwest, a wheat-growing region, the breadbasket of a very young nation. It was part of the rise of Buffalo. It was all the things it has been since those long-ago days. Now 722 Sycamore Street lies fallow.

And Eddie? There is a keen, inarticulate patience about him as he sits in a shell-backed chair in the dusk. Eddie's neighbors are contractors and volunteer firemen. They barbecue, build, and renovate. They root for the Bills, the Sabres, the Bisons. They shoot hoops in the driveway, take the boat to the river, drive the RV to Yellowstone in July. Eddie practices patience, also faith. Tonight he watches the Thruway. He takes a swallow of beer, and his voice falls still in the darkness.

Whenever Eddie and Renee eat out, he is recognized. Old customers stop by to shake hands, though there are fewer and fewer to remember him now. At McPartlan's, The Red Carpet, The Carriage House, and The Protocol —Jerry Pelczynski's restaurant on Transit—the owners greet Eddie as one of their kind. Eddie looks over the room with a professional eye, and he is always happy when business is good. He orders the fish fry.

Notes

PAGE

Epigraph **"Buffalo is not a snobbish city"**: quoted in Richard C. Brown and Bob Watson, *Buffalo: Lake City in Niagara Land* (Woodland Hills, CA: Windsor Publications, 1984), 112.

EDDIE

18   **"one of the loveliest burial places"**: Captain Willard Glazier, *Peculiarities of American Cities* (Philadelphia: Hubbard Brothers, 1885), 62.

21   **"Mediterranean Sea of America"**: Brown and Watson, *Buffalo: Lake City in Niagara Land*, 108.

THOMAS

35   **"The saloon keeper of a Slavic group"**: Emily Greene Balch, *Our Slavic Fellow Citizens* (NY: Arno, 1969; reprint of 1910 edition), 308–309.

44   **a million Poles**: Victor Greene, "Poles," in *The Harvard Encyclopedia of American Ethnic Groups*, ed. Stephan Thernstrom (Cambridge, Mass.: Belknap Press, 1980), 791.

a Latinized version of "Halich": Piotr S. Wandycz, *The Lands of Partitioned Poland, 1795–1918* (Seattle: University of Washington Press, 1979), 11.

half were Polish: *Austrian Poland* (London: H.M. Stationery Office, 1920; Handbooks Prepared under the Direction of the Historical Section of the Foreign Office, No. 46), 9.

45   **"For the most part"**: Francis E. Clark, *Old Homes of New Americans* (Boston: Houghton Mifflin, 1913), 62.

"the glory of snow-crowned mountain peaks": William F. Bailey, "Life in Eastern Galicia," *The Fortnightly Review*, July 1915, 105.

"have a talent for sleep": Ibid., 97.

"there are about two dogs": Ibid., 100.

"the Poles are generally regarded": Ibid., 104.

45 **"Nowhere else do [Poles]"**: Balch, *Our Slavic Fellow Citizens*, 125.
"In Galicia . . . the struggle": Reports of the Immigration Commission, 1907–1910, Volume 4, *Emigration Conditions in Europe* (Washington: Government Printing Office), 381.

46 **"the peasant lives . . . other provinces"**: Ibid., 370.
"their only oppressor": Lion Phillimore, *In the Carpathians* (NY: Henry Holt, 1912), 84.
world monopoly: Wandycz, *Lands of Partitioned Poland*, 277.
"characterized by chemical indifference": *Encyclopedia Britannica*, eleventh edition.
"only 7 factories": Wandycz, *Lands of Partitioned Poland*, 277.
"great misery": Ibid., 222.

47 **109 percent**: Andrzej Brozek, *Polish Americans, 1854–1939* (Warsaw: Interpress, 1985), 20.
1890 census: Balch, *Our Slavic Fellow Citizens*, 46.
300 "agriculturists": *Austrian Poland*, 11.
"A peasant's holding": *Emigration Conditions in Europe*, 365.

48 **"Of all the agricultural properties"**: Balch, *Our Slavic Fellow Citizens*, 138.
"Buffalo's large Polish and Italian population": *The Fact Book of Buffalo* (ca. 1928).
"labor not requiring long apprenticeship": Ibid.

49 **"the houses are without improvements"**: Reports of the Immigration Commission, 1907–1910, Volume 26, *Immigrants in Cities* (Washington: Government Printing Office, 1911), 614.
"good housekeeping should be regarded": Ibid., 645–46.
"life is a narrow valley": Henry Adams, *The Education of Henry Adams* (Boston: Houghton Mifflin, 1961), 64.
"Marked scientific progress": *Buffalo Express Pictorial Yearbook and Calendar for 1888*, July 16 entry.

51 **"hard-faced men"**: Mabel Dodge Luhan, *Intimate Memories* (NY: Harcourt, Brace, 1933), 3.

54 **"Buffalo, the one uniquely cosmopolitan city"**: Daniel J. Sweeney, ed., *History of Buffalo and Erie County, 1914–1919* (Buffalo: 1919). Most of the details in this paragraph are taken from this work.
"Buffalo Women Face the Hun": Title of Chapter L, ibid.
"Ma name Tony Monanco": Ibid., 76.

55 **"Never before in the history of the world"**: Ibid., 49.

JULIA

65 **"This is a great country":** Department of Commerce and Labor, Bureau of Immigration and Naturalization, *Information for Immigrants Concerning the United States: Its Opportunities, Government and Institutions*, prepared by the National Society of the Sons of the American Revolution (Washington: Government Printing Office, 1908).

73 **Chicago is a Poland:** This phrase, *"Cykago* is a Poland," is quoted in Brozek, *Polish Americans, 1854–1939*, 171.

75 **"charging 25 cents for a sight of the pig":** *Dictionary of American Regional English*, ed. Frederic G. Cassidy (Cambridge, Mass.: Belknap Press, 1985).

84 **"scores of tempting and appetizing food products":** *Buffalo's Text Book* (Buffalo: Robert W. Elmes, 1924), 57.

85 **"After a good wine, a good horse!":** Quoted in Fred Jablonski, "The Dynamics of an East Buffalo Ethnic Neighborhood" (Master's Thesis, SUNY Buffalo, 1976), 24.
    "a capacity of 1,500,000 pounds": Ibid., 43.

ARARAT

88 **"I silently contemplated":** Alexis de Tocqueville, *Democracy in America*, translated by George Lawrence (NY: Perennial Library, 1988), 284.
    "Corporations are immortal": Richard Hooker, *Laws of Ecclesiastical Polity*, ed. W. Speed Hill (Cambridge, Mass.: Belknap Press, 1977), I, 10, 8.
    "separation between past": Quoted in Jeremy Bernstein, "Besso," *The New Yorker*, February 27, 1989, 92.

89 **pop. 2,412:** Mark Goldman, *High Hopes: The Rise and Decline of Buffalo, New York* (Albany: SUNY Press, 1983), 50.
    Ararat: See Robert W. Bingham, *Niagara Frontier Miscellany* (Buffalo: Buffalo Historical Society, 1947), 67 ff.
    "Citizen of the United States . . .": Hyam Horowitz, "Ararat on the Great Lakes," *Inland Seas* (Summer, 1948; vol. 4, no. 2), 120–23.

90 **"Hope is not the forerunner of certainty":** Mordecai Noah, *Gleanings from a Gathered Harvest* (NY: H. Long, 1847), 107.
    "While the earth remaineth": Genesis 8:22; King James Version.

91 **"When the war of 1812 broke out":** Glazier, *Peculiarities of American Cities*, 58.
    "unequally poised": Dickens, *Oliver Twist*.
    "a comely noble face": George W. Hosmer, "The Physiognomy

of Buffalo," Annual Address Delivered Before the Buffalo Historical Society, January 13, 1864, 4.

92   **"Would that a painter"**: Ibid., 2.
"God has made Buffalo": Quoted in Brown and Watson, *Buffalo: Lake City in Niagara Land*, 18.
"buxom Buffalonian": Henry Graff, ed., *The Presidents: A Reference History* (NY: Scribner's, 1984), 338.

93   **"Buffalo is a point"**: Frank Severance, ed., *Millard Fillmore Papers* (Buffalo: Buffalo Historical Society, 1907), I, 52.
"cool in summer": *Buffalo Means Business* (n.d. but before 1941).
"The poet says": Severance, *Millard Fillmore Papers*, I, 411.
"Buffalo! Is it not a strange name for a city?": Ibid., II, 71.
"Buffalo in the progress of history": Ibid., II, 68.

94   **"I was here in the autumn of 1835"**: Hosmer, "The Physiognomy of Buffalo," 8.
"Not many years": Robert Bingham, *The Cradle of the Queen City* (Buffalo: Buffalo Historical Society, 1931), 5.

95   **"Thus they passed"**: Ibid., 39.
"View of Buffalo Harbor": See Frank Severance, ed., *The Picture Book of Earlier Buffalo* (Buffalo: Buffalo Historical Society, 1912).

96   **"the most eastern west"**: Glazier, *Peculiarities of American Cities*, 59.
"Supply from the West": Fred Jablonski, "The Dynamics of an East Buffalo Ethnic Neighborhood," 10.
"I wouldn't give the Americans": Quoted in André Jardin, *Tocqueville: A Biography* (NY: Farrar, Straus, Giroux, 1988), 133.
"Buffalo will double its population": "The City of Buffalo," *The Forum*, March 1895.

97   **"If the Thames had a fall"**: C. E. Burk, compiler, *Buffalo To-Day: Industrial and Commercial* (Buffalo: Chamber of Commerce, 1905–1906), 5.

98   **"wholly existential"**: Jane Jacobs, *The Economy of Cities* (NY: Vintage, 1970), 141.

99   **"Niagara Falls is an inexhaustible mine of wealth"**: Goldman, *High Hopes*, 133.

100 **"to illustrate a portion"**: Burk, *Buffalo To-Day*, 5.

101 **"The way to insure the prosperity of Buffalo"**: Goldman, *High Hopes*, 131.

102 **"To assure Buffalo of the future growth"**: *Buffalo: America's Gateway to and from the Great North West, 1920 Year Book* (Buffalo: J. W. Clement Co., 1920), 7.
"When a project is on hand": Goldman, *High Hopes*, 129.
"grinding away steadily": *Greater Buffalo and Niagara Frontier, Commercial and Industrial Illustrated*, 1914.

103 **"There are as many miles"**: "The City of Buffalo," *The Forum*, March 1895.

"the champion residential street": Ellen Taussig, *Your Host, Peter Gust of the Park Lane Restaurant: His Story* (Boston: Herman Publishing, 1979), 47.

"Boost-a-Grams": These appear in *Municipal Buffalo, 1921* (Civic Section of the 1921 City Directory), and in *Buffalo: America's Gateway*, 80.

105 **"The City of Buffalo has all the favorable conditions"**: William Thurstone, *A Sketch of the Commerce, Industries, and Resources of Buffalo* (1883).

"The Tanning Industry is destined": *Buffalo: America's Gateway*, 33.

"among the wastes of time": Shakespeare, Sonnet XII, 10.

106 **"where merchants most do congregate"**: *Merchant of Venice*, I, iii, 50.

107 **"Man had translated himself"**: *The Education of Henry Adams*, 381.

"of inspiring accomplishment": This and the following quotations and all information about Buffalo's Centennial are taken from the "Official Program and Guide, Buffalo Centennial 1832–1932" (published by the Buffalo Centennial Committee, 1932).

108 **"strange invisible perfume"**: Shakespeare, *Antony and Cleopatra*, II, ii, 217.

"Buffalo has 3,000 manufacturers": *Fact Book of Buffalo* (ca. 1928).

109 **"serene confidence"**: The words of Mayor George Buck in the Buffalo Directory Civic Section (1920), 23.

117 **eighty-one minutes**: Brown and Watson, *Buffalo: Lake City in Niagara Land*, 41–42.

EDDIE

118 **"The days are distinct"**: Elias Canetti, *The Human Province* (NY: Farrar, Straus, Giroux, 1978), 3.

AN INNOCENT POPULATION

149 **"The ideas of people in general are not raised higher"**: Nathaniel Hawthorne, *The American Notebooks* (Ohio State University Press, 1972), 24.

"unusually rich in comets": William Schuyler, *The American Year Book: A Record of Events and Progress, Year 1947* (NY: Thomas Nelson & Sons, 1948), 705.

"At no time in history": Ibid., 508.

149 **"very few large bridges"**: Ibid., 714.

150 **"It was downright abnormal of Joe"**: *Saturday Evening Post*, January 11, 1947.

151 **"even Hirohito would like to be holding American War Bonds"**: Ad in *The Railroad Workers Journal* (Official Organ of the Railroad Yardmasters of North America, published in Buffalo), March 1946.
"Even after she got better": Ibid., February 1946.
"What first gave you the notion": Ad for the *Saturday Evening Post*, January 18, 1947.

152 **"There was never a better time"**: Walter Lippmann, *The Essential Lippmann*, edited by Clinton Rossiter and James Lare (Cambridge, Mass.: Harvard University Press, 1963), 77.
"are in the pleasant predicament": Quoted in Eric F. Goldman, *The Crucial Decade—and After: America, 1945–1960* (NY: Vintage, 1960), 14.

153 **"rubble heap," "charnel house"**: Winston Churchill's phrases, quoted in ibid., 66. Most of the facts in the succeeding paragraphs are taken from Schuyler, *The American Year Book*; Thomas Leonard, ed., *Day by Day: The Forties* (NY: Facts on File, 1977); or the *1948 Britannica Book of the Year: Events of 1947* (Chicago: Encyclopedia Britannica, 1948).

155 **"Few other than those highly trained"**: *Liquor Store & Dispenser*, May 1947 cover story.

158 **142 million**: *1948 Britannica Book of the Year.*

160 **a dirigible had flown over Buffalo:** The photograph from which this description is taken can be found in the Bob Hauser Collection in the Buffalo and Erie County Historical Society.

162 **"flying disc," "flat and round"**: Leonard, ed., *Day by Day: The Forties.*

166 **"Strange Forces Hold the Universe Together"**: *Saturday Evening Post*, January 11, 1947.
"The Atomic Age Has Arrived": This appeared as the advertisement on the inside back cover of the program for the September 26, 1948, football game between the Buffalo Bills and the San Francisco 49ers, a program in which George & Eddie's also placed an ad: "Fine Food: Choice Liquor: Dancing: Television."

168 **"It Takes 8 Tons of Freight to K.O. 1 Jap"**: A photograph of this billboard appears in Mark Harris, Franklin Mitchell, and Steven Schechter, *The Homefront: American During World War II* (NY: Putnam, 1984), 40.

169 **9,700 pounds**: Richard Rhodes, *The Making of the Atomic Bomb* (NY: Simon and Schuster, 1986), 701.
"We must assume that with the passage of only a little time":

Quoted in Paul Boyer, *By the Bomb's Early Light* (NY: Pantheon, 1985), 5.

169 **"Seldom, if ever, has a war ended"**: Ibid., 7.

170 **"[One] forgets the effect on Japan"**: Ibid., 6.
   "that it has come to us instead of to our enemies": Ibid., 6.

174 **"the first Civil Defense field exercise"**: The details and quotations in this paragraph are taken from Taussig, *Your Host, Peter Gust of the Park Lane Restaurant*, 131 ff.

THE FALLS

175 **"In that long—long time, never still for a single moment"**: Abraham Lincoln, "Fragment on Niagara Falls," in *Abraham Lincoln: Speeches and Writings, 1832–1858* (NY: Library of America, 1989), 224.

179 **"sordid and hopeless elements," "men out of the ranks"**: Woodrow Wilson, *A History of the American People* (NY: Harper and Brothers, 1902), vol. 5, 212.

185 **"On his left sank the cliffs"**: Francis Parkman, *La Salle and the Discovery of the Great West* (Boston: Little, Brown, 1907), 139.

ACKNOWLEDGMENTS

The Last Fine Time was written in part during a grant year provided by the National Endowment for the Arts. Most of the research for this book was conducted at the Buffalo and Erie County Historical Society, the New York Public Library, where the Frederick Lewis Allen room was made available to me, and the Widener Library, Harvard University. I would like to thank the staffs in each of those places for their generous assistance. My thanks go to all those former residents of Buffalo's East Side who indulged my curiosity, as well as to Kate Bucknell and John Klinkenborg, who read early versions of this book. My gratitude also belongs to Bob Gottlieb and Josselyn Simpson of The New Yorker, to Joan Keener and especially to Bobbie Bristol and Flip Brophy, who never once thought twice about this project.

ABOUT THE AUTHOR

VERLYN KLINKENBORG was born in Colorado and raised in Iowa and California. He has a B.A. from Pomona College and a Ph.D. from Princeton University, and teaches creative writing at Harvard University. He is the author of *Making Hay,* and his work has appeared in *The New Yorker, Smithsonian, The New Republic, Esquire, Harper's,* and *New England Monthly.* He lives with his wife, Regina Wenzek, in Massachusetts and Montana. Eddie Wenzek is his father-in-law.